D0122063

ALSO BY JONATHAN YARDLEY

Ring: A Biography of Ring Lardner
Our Kind of People: The Story of an American Family
Out of Step: Notes from a Purple Decade
States of Mind: A Personal Journey Through the Mid-Atlantic

MISFIT

MISƑIT

THE STRANGE LIFE
OF
FREDERICK EXLEY

JONATHAN YARDLEY

RANDOM HOUSE
NEW YORK

Copyright © 1997 by Jonathan Yardley
All rights reserved under International and Pan-American Copyright Conventions. Published in the United States by Random House, Inc., New York, and simultaneously in Canada by Random House of Canada Limited, Toronto.

Grateful acknowledgment is made to the following for permission to reprint previously published material:

Random House, Inc.: Excerpts from *A Fan's Notes* by Frederick Exley. Copyright © 1968 by Frederick Exley. Copyright renewed 1996 by Frances Exley Brown and Constance O'Neill. Excerpts from *Pages from a Cold Island* by Frederick Exley. Copyright © 1974, 1975 by Frederick Exley. Excerpts from *Last Notes from Home* by Frederick Exley. Copyright © 1988 by Frederick Exley. Reprinted by permission of Random House, Inc.

Watertown Daily Times: Excerpts from articles that appeared in the *Watertown Daily Times*. Reprinted by permission of the *Watertown Daily Times*.

Inside Sports: Excerpts from an article by Frederick Exley from the November 1981 issue of INSIDE SPORTS. Copyright © 1981 by INSIDE SPORTS. Reprinted with permission.

Library of Congress Cataloging-in-Publication Data
Yardley, Jonathan.
Misfit : the strange life of Frederick Exley / by Jonathan
Yardley. — 1st ed.
p.   cm.
ISBN 0-679-43949-8 (hard cover)
1. Exley, Frederick—Biography.   2. Novelists, American—20th
century—Biography.   3. Exley, Frederick.   I. Title.
PS3555.X58Z97 1997
813'.54—dc21
[B]   96-51737

Random House website address: http://www.randomhouse.com/
Printed in the United States of America on acid-free paper
2 3 4 5 6 7 8 9
First Edition

Book design by Bernard Klein

For my beloved children
Jim and Theo
Bill and Eileen

Listen, you son of a bitch, life isn't all a goddam football game!
You won't always get the girl! Life is rejection and pain and
loss. . . .

A Fan's Notes

PROLOGUE

BIOGRAPHY IS A VAIN AND FOOLHARDY UNDERTAKING. ITS
essential conceit, that the unimaginable distance between
two human beings can be crossed, is insupportable; each of
us is inherently unknowable. The biographer may be able to
locate his subject in place and time—to describe the clothes
he wore, the food he ate, the jobs he held, the opinions he
expressed—but that subject's inner essence is, by its very
nature, forever inaccessible.

If this is true of all those about whom biographers write,
it is true a thousand times over of Frederick Earl Exley. He
was the most elusive and mysterious of men; he lived on
another planet, if not in another universe. To write a conventional account of his life would be pointless, not just
because that life was so thoroughly unconventional but
because he left so few of the convenient signposts by which
biographers customarily mark their subjects' progress. He
rarely spoke about intimate matters, so no one who knew
him can testify about them with authority. Until late in his

life, he saved almost nothing, so documentary spoor is scant. Anyplace he hung his hat was home; he had many addresses, most belonging to other people, and he rarely bothered to record them on his correspondence, with the consequence that even the most mundane of biographers' questions—where was he, and when?—is often, in his case, quite literally unanswerable. More important, it is of no consequence. The life's journey that Fred Exley made was interior, and no compendium of biographical trivia, however interesting, can help us track it. We must look elsewhere, which is what I have tried to do in the pages that follow.

Fred was a professional writer, though only one of his three books will long remain in print. His chief claim upon our attention is his own account of his life, that "fictional memoir" called *A Fan's Notes,* which is not merely a classic of American literature but one to which readers have responded with as much intensity as Fred brought to the writing of it. Where did that book come from? The question has haunted many of these readers, along with its corollary: Is the "Fred Exley" depicted therein a real or a fictional character? Though neither of these questions is susceptible to conclusive answers, I have addressed myself to them herein and have reached certain judgments that are, I hope, reasonably persuasive.

In addition, Fred's life both paralleled and embodied, however accidentally and oddly, the lives of many American writers of his time. There are patterns and themes in Fred's life and work that can be found in the lives and works of his contemporaries, so it is—or so at least it seems to me—possible to view him as a case study as well as a discrete individual. No attempt will be made to stake out larger claims

for Fred than the facts warrant, but I think that a brief narrative of his life will tell us a few things about what it means
to be a writer in America as well as what it was to be Frederick Earl Exley.

I will elaborate upon this aspect of Fred's story presently,
but must pause for a moment to discharge one small duty
that has puzzled and vexed me since I first decided to
undertake this project. Fred Exley and I never met, and I
would not claim to have been his "friend" in the customary
sense of the word, yet we were friendly in a way and
touched each other's lives as well; had this connection not
existed, it would never have occurred to me to write this
book. However minor my role in Fred's life may have been,
it was part of his story. Because I prefer to keep myself out of
what is, after all, his biography and not mine, I have decided
to tell my end of the tale at the outset and leave it at that,
keeping the first-person singular out of the narrative, saying
only that I believe others will recognize, in my reaction to *A
Fan's Notes* and the feelings that book provoked about its
author, reactions and emotions of their own.

I came to *A Fan's Notes* almost entirely by accident. In the
late summer of 1968 I was twenty-nine years old and an editorial writer at the *Daily News* in Greensboro, North Carolina, as well as its book editor. I was packing my bags to go
off to Harvard for an academic year on a Nieman Fellowship, a postgraduate stipend awarded annually to a dozen
American journalists with the provision that they broaden
their minds in any way they like rather than merely add to
their academic credentials. The idea is that on a Nieman
year one does a lot of high-level talking and a lot of mind-
expanding reading. With the latter in mind I poked around
in my stack of review copies and tossed several into a box,

one being a book that seemed to be about professional football, for which in those days I carried a high-octane torch, a book that came with the surprisingly enthusiastic endorsement of its publisher—surprising, that is, since in those days no one took books about sports seriously in any terms, least of all literary ones.

For weeks *A Fan's Notes* stood on a shelf in the apartment my young family had rented in Cambridge. We were sociable and often had other members of the little Nieman community around for dinner or parties. On one of these occasions Mike McGrady, who was then a columnist for *Newsday,* picked up the book and asked to borrow it. A couple of days later he reported about his reading in the most ecstatic terms, which led Paul Hemphill, then a columnist for *The Atlanta Constitution,* to ask that McGrady pass the book along to him.

Thus *A Fan's Notes* began its legendary passage through the Nieman Class of 1968–69: legendary, that is, in the mind of Fred Exley, who in his first letter to me referred (I hope with a sardonic smile) to "the intellectual elite—you, McGrady and those other Nieman fellows who were so kind to me." Perhaps a half dozen of my classmates read it; I was immersed in a graduate seminar on the work of William Faulkner and didn't come up for air until the spring, but the fervor with which my friends discussed Exley and his book made me look forward to it with appetite and curiosity.

All the members of the Nieman class that year were between their late twenties and late thirties; all but one were male; all but one were white. We were reasonably well educated, intensely connected to the daily life of our work, rather bumptious and boisterous, and more than casually interested in our own interior lives. We were, that is to say, people likely to respond to *A Fan's Notes* in personal and passionate ways, because it was the testament of a man who, although slightly older than most of us, saw the world and himself through eyes we recognized because they were at once very much like our own yet so much keener than ours, and pierced so much more deeply into whatever they encountered.

When at last in the spring of 1969 I read the book myself, my reaction was every bit as ardent as my friends' had been. This was not because my life had been much like the one depicted in *A Fan's Notes*. I shared Exley's ardor for professional football and, in those younger and stronger days, for distilled spirits, but otherwise we were quite different people. I was a steady wage earner on a career track pointed in a slightly upward direction, the father of two young sons to whom I was intensely devoted, and, on the whole, more conventional than not in habits if not all attitudes. Much that I read in *A Fan's Notes* struck me as alien. Yet beneath the surface differences in our lives, I recognized that Exley was writing about matters that troubled me as they did him, particularly—this being a subject about which it is no longer fashionable to talk—the inner struggles attendant to being a white middle-class male in late-twentieth-century America. I also felt a powerful sympathy and empathy for Exley's apprehension that his would be a life unrecognized and unrewarded. I understood, as Exley so memorably wrote, "and could not bear to understand, that it was my destiny . . . to sit in the stands with most men and acclaim others. It was my fate, my destiny, my end, to be a fan."

I took *A Fan's Notes* back to Greensboro when it was time to return to the real world. In the fall of 1969, when the paperback edition of *A Fan's Notes* was published, I wrote a piece about it for my newspaper. I lamented what I described as the indifferent reception the hardcover edition had received, in response to which I got an irritated letter from Exley's editor at Harper & Row, David Segal, taking me to task for overlooking what he called the "extraordinarily large and favorable press" that, he said, the book had received.

Precisely who was right in this exchange seems to me even now a moot question, but in any event I was not finished with *A Fan's Notes.* By 1974 I had moved to *The Miami Herald* and had become a regular contributor to the literary pages of *The New Republic,* for which in the spring of 1975 I wrote a "Reconsideration" of *A Fan's Notes,* a piece motivated chiefly by my unchanged and ever-stronger conviction that the book had as yet received nothing approximating its proper due.

It is at this point that Fred entered my life directly. I don't know how he learned that I was working on this piece— probably through McGrady or Hemphill, both of whom had by then interviewed him—but one night my phone rang and a slurred voice greeted me. It was of course Fred, and it was the first of many such calls by which my life was to be blessed and cursed in the two decades to come.

Fred's boozy phone calls were the wide net that he cast out into the world, whether from Watertown or Alexandria Bay or Hawaii or one of his many haunts in Florida. The recipients must have numbered in the hundreds, and judging by the testimony I have received from others, all had roughly the same experience. Unlike many who are inspired to use the telephone under the influence of alcohol, Fred did not subject those listening to him to abuse and he did not wallow in self-pity, at least not in my experience. He simply wanted to talk; he did *not* want to listen. A conversation with Fred was a one-way affair in which the party at the other end was lucky to squeeze in a word or a phrase, none of which added up to anything more than punctuation marks.

"Talking" with Fred was thus a frustrating and occasionally maddening experience, but this did not make me enjoy it any the less. I was honored by his calls, honored that he considered me his friend even though, as it turned out, we never actually met. I'm sure the reader can imagine how I felt when, in the course of one of his ramblings, he asked if I would agree to be his literary executor. I said to my wife once the call finally ended that this was an honor I never actually would enjoy, as indeed I did not, but in its peculiar way it was an honor all the same.

A couple of years later my first book, a biography of Ring Lardner, was heading toward publication. It was being published by Random House and edited by Bob Loomis, who had become Fred's editor following David Segal's untimely and much-mourned death. A set of bound proofs was sent to Fred in hopes of what editors call a "comment" and what everyone else calls a "blurb." Fred responded immediately, with a couple of sentences that were not mere flattery but genuine kindness and, I believe, genuine empathy for the book and its author. I suppose a cynic would say that Fred was buttering up his editor and a reviewer, but not for a moment would I agree.

Fred was the first novelist of genuine distinction with whom I struck up something on the order of a friendship, however odd it may have been. Since 1975 I have made several such friendships, and I have become incalculably less awestruck by writers than I was then, but my telephonic friendship with Fred is something that I still treasure. When word came to me in 1992 of his death I was not surprised—if anything, I was surprised that he had managed to live so long—but I was genuinely grieved to know that I would never again hear another Exley monologue.

Between 1975 and 1992 I wrote several pieces about Fred's work: the aforementioned Greensboro and *New Republic* ones, as well as reviews of both *Pages from a Cold Island* and *Last Notes from Home,* and an essay about the man and his life that appeared a few days after his death. My reviews of Fred's second and third books were far more positive than my actual judgments of them, but I believed that Fred was a writer of such deep and unique talent that he should be protected and encouraged at all costs; in this, I discovered as I began to research his life, I was anything but alone.

I also wrote about Fred when, in 1982, I assembled a list of the works of American twentieth-century fiction that I regard as essential reading. I included *A Fan's Notes* in that list and would do so again should anyone ask me to reassess my judgments. This apparently meant a great deal to Fred, for he sent out many copies of the piece, one of which went to his friend David Markson, the novelist:

> Have you . . . heard about this Washington Post article and the furor it's causing? Although Yardley won the Pulitzer for criticism last year, and I expect this gives him partial license to say anything he damn pleases, this like any other was bound to elicit approbation and catcalls, agreement and jeers, approval and disbelief. Yardley's main omission (other than Markson, of course), it seems to me, is not Henry

James but Nabokov, whose absence Yardley doesn't even deign to explain. For all that, I'm glad he did that to Mailer and Heller and to "all them New Yorker guys" and I was of course pleased to be included in such formidable company.

Though no one knows better than I the fundamental silliness and evanescence of such exercises in journalistic list-making—the unpardonable omission of *Lolita* underscores the point—that list came at a time when Fred's self-confidence was low. It seems to have given him a boost, or so at least I hope.

So much for me. Now I would like to suggest three broad themes that are self-evident in Fred's life and important in the larger literary culture of which he was a part. I hope that these will emerge as the story of Fred's life unfolds, but I have not harped upon them therein. I prefer to discuss them now by way of background and then to tell Fred's story simply as what it is: a story.

Fred Exley spent much of his writing life in remote places, but he did not write in a vacuum. He was influenced by many of the same things that influenced other writers and he confronted many of the same problems they did. Specifically, he suffered under the burden of the one-book syndrome, which is itself an outgrowth of the culture of autobiography; he was torn between a longing for celebrity and fame in the most superficial senses of both words and, on the other hand, his deeper knowledge that the work itself was all that really mattered. It seems to me that in any discussion of Fred Exley these questions—productivity, autobiography, fame—are absolutely essential.

All of these themes as thus briefly described are in some measure negative judgments, or reservations, or qualms, about Fred: assessments of how his work was limited rather than how it was successful. So let me emphasize that in my judgment *A Fan's Notes* is one of the few monuments of postwar American fiction. It stands, in its unique and inimitable way, with the best work of Ralph Ellison, Eudora Welty, Peter Taylor, Bernard Malamud, Saul Bellow, Flannery O'Connor, John Cheever—all the other writers of the best books of our age. *A Fan's Notes* may not live forever, but I expect it to live for a long time, which is to say that it will meet one of the inescapable tests by which real literature is measured. As I will argue when the time comes to discuss the book in detail, it meets other tests as well.

It remains, though, that when Fred died at the age of sixty-three, *A Fan's Notes* was, to all intents and purposes, his only book. No doubt some graduate student of English, desperate for a doctoral subject that will separate him or her from the crowd, will look into *Pages from a Cold Island* and *Last Notes from Home* and find reason to honor them with fifty thousand words of exegesis. Out of such efforts are doctorates won and tenure achieved, but they do not alter the essential truth, which is that Fred's second and third books are afterthoughts, or footnotes, to his first. They were written—I know this from the books themselves and from all those phone calls—not merely honestly but desperately, because Fred, who knew he was working against a rapid clock, wanted nothing so much as to write another book that would reach the same heights he had achieved in *A Fan's Notes*. These later books must not be taken lightly if for no other reason than that Fred wrote them and that they are the final proof of his inability to repeat one of the singular accomplishments of American literature. But they must be accepted for the honorable failures that in fact they are.

This is not a bad thing; it is a very American thing. The one-book great writer, or the one-book not-so-great writer, is among our most common and characteristic literary phenomena; the phrase "one-book writer" is so often used that it should be included in our glossaries of literary terms. Usually it is employed pejoratively, as in "He's just a one-book writer," or "He has only one book in him." The implicit assumption is that the person who can write only one good book is not a writer to be reckoned with.

Are we to say this of Ralph Ellison? It is true beyond doubt that he published just one novel. Does this somehow make *Invisible Man* less than we once thought it was? Of course it doesn't. *Invisible Man* is one of the great American novels, perhaps the greatest, a masterpiece pure and simple. We may be disappointed that Ellison did not give us another novel, sorry that he did not assemble a shelf of books such as, say, Faulkner's or Dreiser's, but this is a matter of our expectations rather than Ellison's achievement. We forget this when we chastise our one-book writers, and in so doing we do them no good service.

There are several reasons why so many American writers have only one book in them. One is that it is very hard to be a writer of serious fiction in this country, not merely because we have so little respect for such work but because we throw up so many distractions in the way of it. All the hullabaloo attendant to writing a book to which other people respond intensely can be hugely flattering and can make it difficult to get on with one's work. Other, younger, far less gifted writers than Fred have become so caught up in the social whirl that passes in New York City for the literary life that they failed to expand or deepen whatever literary gifts they may have possessed. In Fred's case, he genuinely liked being the center of attention at places like his favorite Greenwich Village saloon, the Lion's Head, places that did nothing to discourage him from the boozing to which he lost so many hours.

Successful first books also raise expectations that can be painfully hard to meet; they become deterrents to writing itself. *A Fan's Notes* never was a best-seller, but it accumulated a cult, the members of which wanted nothing so much as a second *A Fan's Notes,* and a third, and a fourth. Fred, a gregarious man in his fashion, got to know many of the members of this cult and was subjected at first hand to the hopes and longings they had attached to him. One can only guess at how much of an obstacle this presented, but my hunch is that it was considerable. The most telling evidence is that both *Pages from a Cold Island* and *Last Notes from Home* are transparent attempts to repeat the formula Fred had devised in *A Fan's Notes.* Having written a book about yearning for glory as achieved by Frank Gifford, Fred went on to write two more books about yearning for glory as achieved by, first, Edmund Wilson, and, second, Fred's own brother, Bill. What was natural and intrinsic in *A Fan's Notes* was artificial and strained in the second and third books, because they were books Fred thought he ought to write rather than books he simply had to write.

But the most important reason why one-book writers are so common in twentieth-century American fiction—the reason why Fred Exley was a one-book writer—has to do with the second of these three themes. Whether *A Fan's Notes* is really a novel or really a memoir is, in the end, unimportant, but this much is certain: it is a work of autobiography. Its sole inspiration and its sole raw material are the same: the inner and outer lives of the man who wrote it. Because Fred Exley was observant and smart and funny, because his imaginative life was rich and original, *A Fan's Notes* is itself rich and original, but it also contains the seeds of its author's literary self-destruction.

The problem with autobiographical fiction—the problem with most serious American fiction of the past three quarters of a century—is that its limits are those of its authors' psyches and experiences. There is little evidence that Fred was genuinely interested in anyone or anything except himself. Those one-way telephone conversations suggest as much, as do all three books, in which people other than Fred matter not for who they are and what they do but for how Fred sees them and how he connects with them. His great gift was to make us empathize with him and laugh with him, but his great limitation was that he could not reach beyond himself to expand the possibilities of his fiction and thus the number of readers with whom it could connect.

If it is true that all of us are born with just a few arrows in our quivers—that there are only so many things we can do and so many more we cannot—then it is equally true that there are just a few things about ourselves that are of actual or potential interest to others. Each of us has only one story to tell—if, that is, we have been blessed with the storytelling gift—and once this story is told, the writer who cannot go on to other matters is fated to decline and disappointment. The most telling example is to be found in the career of Philip Roth, a prodigiously talented writer who has told his own story over and over again, all the time insisting against all the evidence that he is *not* telling his own story, in the process becoming so self-absorbed that his life's work shrinks in importance even as it grows in bulk.

If such creatures as authors and critics still exist a century from now, they will look back on the American literary culture of the twentieth century and conclude that self-absorption was its dominant characteristic. This is a direct consequence of the influence of James Joyce and Sigmund Freud. I have no reason to believe that Fred Exley had more than a passing interest in either—he did use a quotation from Joyce as an epigraph for *Pages from a Cold Island*—but he was inescapably influenced by them. Joyce and Freud are in the atmosphere, floating invisibly all about us, shaping the way we see ourselves and, if we are writers, the way we write.

What they tell us—this is oversimplification, but it is true—is that the self is all, that our proper preoccupation is with our own minds and lives. We should look inside ourselves and see the universe in miniature, and in writing about ourselves we should describe the universe for others. So at least we are to believe, and so to be sure virtually every American writer of literary fiction believes.

Invisible Man and *A Fan's Notes,* those one-book authors' monuments, are novels written from within that do touch universal chords, and our literature would be far poorer without them. The work of Fred Exley's friend William Styron is characterized by a powerful autobiographical impulse that its author has somehow managed to subordinate to the stories of other people; thus it is that in *Sophie's Choice* the narrator and autobiographical figure, Stingo, is vivid yet in the end subordinate to Sophie and her lover, Nathan, just as Scott Fitzgerald's Nick Carraway is subordinate to Jay Gatsby and Daisy Buchanan. Because fiction arises from the writer's individual imagination, it cannot help being autobiographical in some intrinsic way, but that is not *all* it has to be.

One would never know this from most twentieth-century American fiction, especially that of the past quarter century, during which literary fiction has become an industry managed by the university writing schools, assembly lines that churn out writers who have been actively encouraged in the classroom to "write about what you know," good advice that when taken up by inexperienced hands usually turns out to mean "write about yourself." Fred Exley was not really a member of the writing-school subculture, though he did have his flirtations with it, but he was not immune to flattery from those who inhabited it and could not help being influenced by the signals it emits, since they are everywhere in the contemporary literary world. Having written one immensely accomplished autobiographical work, he found nothing to discourage him from trying to do so again, and he found a great deal that prodded him to follow the same path toward what proved to be far less rewarding destinations.

Unfortunately, Fred had said everything he had to say in *A Fan's Notes,* just as Ellison said it all in *Invisible Man;* less famously, Ross Lockridge said it all in *Raintree County* and Thomas Heggen said it all in *Mister Roberts.* Each of these last two committed suicide. Fred and Ellison soldiered on, bravely trying to say other things—Fred in two novels, Ellison in many fine essays—but they were rendered essentially unproductive by the inherent limitations of their subject matter.

It is true as well that Fred's productivity was limited to a significant extent by alcohol, which to varying degrees has been a constant presence in twentieth-century American literary lives. I have little doubt that Fred felt that drink was essential to being a writer. It was part of his literary self-image, and to the extent that the example of such writers as Faulkner, Wolfe, Fitzgerald and Hemingway beckoned to him, it can be said that Fred's literary aspirations were coconspirators in his alcoholism.

Fred was a drinker; this brought pain to, and exacted other costs upon, those who were closest to him. I am sorry for this, and I know that he was, too. But as I wrote in my obituary tribute to him, "The boozing was a pity and a waste, but it was his choice and he lived with it, just as he died by it." Fred became the writer he was in large measure because of the drinker he was; his drinking is an important part of the story he told us, and there simply is no getting around that.

I suspect that drinking was also an important element in Fred's ambivalent attitude toward literary celebrity and its distractions. That Fred wanted to be famous is beyond dispute; he wrote a great book about not being famous precisely because he hoped it would make him famous, as in small measure it did. He wanted to be recognized as a writer but he also wanted the company of other writers and literary folk who admired him and made him the center of their coterie. From friends who drank with him I have been given vivid images of Fred in his seat at the bar, nursing his vodka or beer and glorying in the praise of whatever claque had assembled at that particular hour.

The folk who can be found at such gatherings are not really literary and often are not especially interesting. My impression is that Fred knew this intellectually but declined to accept it emotionally. He wanted his own version of

Frank Gifford's applause; although he preferred that it came from people he respected, if it didn't he'd take whatever he could get. Because he had written a book about subjects of interest to many journalists and had done so in a style far higher than what any of them could aspire to, they tended to smother him with veneration and to encourage him in the self-destructive behavior for which he had so powerful a bent. Many of them are amusing fellows, gifted with gab and insouciance; I have no idea what he really thought of them, but I know for a fact that he liked not merely their applause but also, purely and simply, their company.

Fred wanted fame and wasn't above employing devious means of advancing his unsteady march toward it; he knew how to flatter reviewers and profile writers, how to present himself as a personality, how to wheedle money out of publishers and magazine editors. If by some miracle of journalism he had ended up on the cover of *People* magazine—and in 1988 he got close—he would have made snide remarks for the consumption of his entourage, but he would have been secretly, and hugely, thrilled.

Apart from his grand novel, what redeems Fred, after you get through all the sloppiness of his life and the frustrating incompleteness of his literary career, is that he was first and foremost a *writer.* He wanted people to know his name because he wanted them to read his books. Cut away all the booze and the empty sex, all the squandered time and the hot-air phone conversations, and you find yourself left with the essence of the man, which was a writer.

It has been my good fortune to know a number of genuinely serious writers, people for whom writing is the chief if not the only thing in their lives, but I've never known one more serious—more obsessive or fixated—than Fred. He would have rejected every bit of tinsel that the American celebrity machine offers in exchange for respect, for reputation, for *readers*. He wanted money, but he wanted it mainly as a measure of accomplishment, and he didn't want it half so much as he wanted to write all those books that, in the end, did not get written.

Questions of celebrity and reputation gnawed at Fred just as they have at many American writers before and since; you can bet that as ours becomes more and more a celebrity culture those questions will become even more distracting. If Fred ever managed to achieve a reconciliation between ambition and reality, between what he wanted and what he actually got, he left no evidence of it. If anything, the pathetic eagerness with which he promoted *Last Notes from Home* for a Pulitzer Prize suggests that at the end he was ready to settle for praise in any form.

Yet there is no reason for reading his life as a story of disappointment and failure, for holding him up as still another American literary tragedy. For one thing, all the evidence indicates that although he was not a happy man, he had a good deal of fun; I am not one to take that lightly, and anyone otherwise inclined does Fred a disservice. But what really matters is that, on his own terms, Fred was a great success.

How could that be? His books didn't sell well, he never achieved the preeminent literary position he so obviously yearned for, and he died much too soon. This is a *success*? Perhaps not in the usual terms. But in those that really mattered to Fred, he triumphed. Fred believed in the written word and the transcendent importance of the book, and in the end he got what he wanted. He wrote his masterwork because he felt fated to sit in the stands and cheer the exploits of those on the field below, but something funny— something wonderful and deliciously ironic—happened. Fred Exley gave Frank Gifford more than Frank Gifford ever could have given Fred Exley. Fred gave Gifford what only art and the gods can bestow, the gift of immortality. For as long as people read *A Fan's Notes,* Frank Gifford will live in the words of Fred Exley. I think that Fred knew this and that it gave him abiding satisfaction.

So: a decidedly unconventional life, a somewhat unconventional biography. My narrative is chronological, but as matters of importance arise I discuss them in full and subsequently refer to them only briefly, no matter how often they recur. These include Fred's hometown and his father; football; Fred's attitudes toward and relations with women; his drinking; his journalism; most important of all, the "wound" or "rage" around which his existence revolved and out of which his work emerged. After wasting a fair amount of time trying to pinpoint Fred's exact whereabouts at certain periods of his life, I concluded that this was utterly irrelevant to the central purposes of this book and abandoned the search; this will exasperate proponents of laundry-list biography, but I hope it enables this story to move more expeditiously toward its principal goals. What I have written is closer to an informal portrait than a biography as the word is now commonly understood; it seems to me the appropriate form for the subject at hand.

My principal sources have been the written words of Fred Exley and the spoken testimony of the people who knew him; those who provided the latter are identified, with immense gratitude, in the acknowledgments at the end of this book. Any passages in quotation marks that are not otherwise identified are from Fred's published work, unpublished manuscripts or letters. On the assumption that most readers of this biography have come to it out of affection for or interest in *A Fan's Notes,* I have tried to keep direct quotation from that book to a minimum. But quoting selectively from his subject's work is one of a literary biographer's obligations, in addition to which there are things about himself that Fred Exley simply said better in *A Fan's Notes* than anyone else possibly could. So there are passages herein that some readers will find familiar; I trust they will consider it a pleasure to encounter them once again. There are also many passages that even the most ardent members of Fred's cult will not recognize; because it seems to me of paramount importance that his voice be heard as often as possible, my quotations from his letters and other unpublished material, and from his family's and friends' recollections of things he said, are frequent and extensive.

Because I have made every effort to confine this account of Fred's life to narrative and informed speculation—to make it a *story* instead of a *study*—no footnotes or scholarly apparatus are provided, but my working papers and manuscript will be available at the University of Rochester for those having a serious interest in Fred Exley. My sources should be self-evident from the text; additional clutter not merely is unnecessary but would distract us from this book's central mission, which is a search for Fred Exley's heart and mind.

PART ONE

EARL AND CHARLOTTE'S BOY

Charlotte holding Frances and Fred
Family photo

FRED EXLEY WAS A RAMBLER, THE LEAST DOMESTIC OF men. He never owned a house and infrequently rented; family and friends were always ready to take him in, and he never hesitated to accept. Over the years he lived in, or touched down upon, all four corners of the continental United States, as well as many places in between, and he spent a great deal of time in Hawaii, on the island of Lanai. As one of his friends once said, "Chasing Freddie can be quite a job." But if this suggests a certain cosmopolitanism, quite the opposite was true. Fred Exley's world was minuscule, and he never left it.

Even small worlds are made up of many elements; the influences that shaped Fred are numerous and in some cases elusive. But two stand above all others. The first is the place, Watertown, New York, into which he was born. The second is the man, Earl Edward Exley, who was his father. The two cannot be separated, for in Fred's mind Watertown and Earl Exley were in many ways inseparable and interchangeable.

The town is a pleasant but strange place, at once boiler-plate Americana and sui generis. It was settled by whites around 1800; they were drawn there by the Black River, an immense natural power plant that falls one hundred and twelve feet within the city limits, muscling up energy every inch of the way, and by a rich store of natural resources, lumber most particularly. Watertown is "the county seat of Jefferson, one of the biggest dairy-producing regions in New York State." Lake Ontario is a few miles to the west, and the St. Lawrence River is twenty-five miles due north. Watertown is now connected to the rest of the world by its small airport and by Interstate 81, which enters south-central New York State near Binghamton and runs north for nearly two hundred miles through Syracuse and Water-town before ending at Wellesley Island in the St. Lawrence, at the Canadian border; but in Fred's youth only two-lane roads and trains served the town, with the result that the outside world tended to stay away and Watertown tended to hunker down.

Isolation is one of two salient facts about Watertown; the other is winter, which is long, cold and bitter. Together the two shape the town's character. An outsider who knew Fred off and on for years said that he had "the Watertown look," defined as "sort of stunted." This was said with tongue only half in cheek. The populace of Watertown probably offers as much diversity of human physiognomy as that of any place; but its isolation and its endless winters draw people together in an alliance against natural circumstances that is often transformed into an alliance against the rest of the world. To the outsider it almost defies comprehension, for the intimacy in which its members live fosters exaggerated emotion; Watertown people love each other and hate each other with equal ardor, and speak about each other's public and private business with familiarity and affection, passion and censoriousness. To the outsider, listening in on Watertown gossip can be exhausting.

Watertown likes to fancy itself a tough place, facing the world with a pugnacity born of survival against steep odds. "In my hometown, Watertown, N.Y., we say to February sojourners: 'Snow? You call this snow? Wait'll it *really* starts snowing!'" Once in the course of his travels Fred found himself in a Haight-Ashbury bar whose owner, Paddy Brennon, "was a few years my senior, muscular, a blackly graying, blue-eyed, amiable and funny Irishman" and, it turned out, was himself a native New Yorker. When he learned that Fred was from Watertown,

Paddy Brennon slowly got off his bar stool and stood, staring at me. He carefully removed his half-moon glasses, folded them, delicately put them into their leather case, which he slid into his shirt pocket. In a grand Irish flourish he took his right arm and swept all the newspapers with his precious racing dope all over the floor. He gravely slammed his hands onto his hipbones and smiled abruptly, showing a lot of rather-too-perfectly even white teeth. Although it wasn't anywhere near five, he pointed at his glass of distilled water and said, "Cutty 12 and ice, Hickey," then ordered a round for the house. He turned back to me. "Have I ever heard of Watertown? *Have I ever heard of Watertown?*" Paddy said it in the way guys say: *Is the Pope Catholic?* "Hey, Hickey, did I ever hear of Watertown?" "Yeah, Paddy, you hearduh Watertown!" Paddy Brennon threw his head back and did some *ho ho hos,* then brought his head down nose-to-nose and eyeball-to-eyeball with mine and sneered spittingly at me.

"Have I ever heard of Watertown? *That's where the god-damn animals are!*"

This brute side was the face that Fred Exley's Watertown liked to present to the world: hard, self-reliant, independent, no-nonsense. It was not a place with much tolerance for feminine qualities, except as they occurred in women. Boys and men were expected to play sports in school, football most particularly, and then go to work for the New York Central or New York Air Brake or Niagara Mohawk or the dairy farms. During Fred's boyhood there were more than fifty industries in or near town, making everything from paper and machinery for manufacturing it to surgical supplies. If a boy or a man was sensitive or artistic by nature he did well to keep it under wraps: go out for the team, hang out with the guys, talk dirty, drink beer.

Drink is—or was during the years that shaped Fred Exley—the curse of Watertown's working classes. Since it is a blue-collar town, the curse is pervasive. So, though to a far lesser extent, is suicide. People turn to both out of the same need, for escape from the obvious—isolation and winter—and perhaps from deeper things: from a sense of being different, from an inability to fit in, from pure and simple fear. Fred Exley, whose entire adult life was spent in self-destructive alcoholism, felt all of those things, and was haunted by them.

"Watertown is not in my marrow, it is my marrow." He never left it, and it never left him. "I knew that where other men look home with longing and affection, I would look home with loathing and rage, and that that loathing would bind me to home as fiercely as love ever does." On the whole he was clearer about the loathing than he was about the reasons for it. Obviously, he was uncomfortable with the town's rigid social and economic structure. At the top was the white Anglo-Saxon Protestant elite, an establishment that not merely ruled Watertown but sent occasional emissaries to the outside: "Secretary of State John Foster Dulles and his brother, Allen, who for a time and as a front for his brother, Foster, headed our Central Intelligence Agency, were from Watertown, the sons of our Presbyterian minister. I shit you not, . . . from Watertown! . . . Watertown and Jefferson County also gave the world Robert Lansing, President Woodrow Wilson's secretary of state. Charles M. Yost, an undersecretary of state and ambassador to the United Nations, was from there." So too was an enterprising store clerk named F. W. Woolworth, who in 1878 set out a table piled high with goods under a sign that read, ANY ARTICLE 5¢; thus was the five-and-dime store born.

These exalted persons and their fellows were known to the less fortunate and more irreverent as the Four Hundred, the ancient term defining the innermost circle of the New York City social elite. The Four Hundred ran most of the town's affairs, from its excellent newspaper, the *Watertown Daily Times,* to its legal and business institutions. Fred, himself white, Anglo-Saxon and Protestant, may have felt that he belonged to this group by right yet had been denied admission for reasons not his own fault. Whatever he thought, he hung out with people whose surnames suggest both his rebellion against the establishment and the heterogeneity of Watertown's citizenry: Jack Scordo, Leo Dephtereos, Gene Renzi, John Doldo, Gordon Phillips.

The last of these was Fred's "best friend": smart, handsome, raffish, hedonistic. Fred and Gordie Phillips met early in their high school years, in plane geometry class, and found common ground at once in their mutual dislike of Watertown's inflexible side. Unlike Fred, Gordie made no gesture toward the local orthodoxy. He ignored football and concentrated, in high school, on girls and drinking, concerning both of which he was uncommonly versed; he believed, according to Fred, "in the consoling power of Fornication," and was often consoled. In time Gordie entered the practice of law, which he pursued for a while in Albany before returning to Watertown. There he entered into practice with another attorney, then went out on his own. Neither of these ventures was smiled upon by the Watertown bar, which was accustomed to shepherding young lawyers through settled firms before allocating them their proper places in the local hierarchy.

Eventually Gordie's disregard for Watertown custom got him into trouble, in a matter that came to symbolize, in Fred's mind, everything that was wrong with his hometown. In 1960 Gordie represented a workingwoman whose signature he needed on a check after settling a case for her. He couldn't find her, closing time at the bank was drawing near, so Fred, who was riding with Gordie, endorsed the check in the client's name "without any misgivings." The woman got her money and Gordie continued to represent her, but an investigation was undertaken by the bar association and after about a year disbarment proceedings were initiated. Under oath, Gordie swore that he had committed the forgery. This was the handle upon which the bar association hung its successful case against Gordie; in *A Fan's Notes* Fred does not mention that Gordie took the rap for him. But this omission meant much less to Gordie than Fred's loyalty. In 1992, at the memorial service for Fred, Gordie told those in attendance: "Many years ago, when I had my troubles with the establishment, some of my friends . . . walked away. But not my friend, Freddie. Whenever Freddie found, or was able to create, a forum, he defended me. He defended me in living rooms, bar rooms, on street corners and, of course, in the pages of *A Fan's Notes*."

Fred claimed that he "took the disbarment harder" than Gordie did, which may have been so in Fred's mind but was not in reality. Gordie was not merely left without a job and unable to practice the work for which he had been trained, but he was separated, his wife was seeking an annulment, and he had three young sons living in Watertown, a place that had just shunned him. It is a tribute to his resourcefulness and determination that he took hard work at manual labor in construction; he subsequently moved to Rochester, started his own construction company and prospered. But this did not serve Fred's needs. He saw Gordie's disbarment as the embodiment of Watertown's insularity and intolerance. In *A Fan's Notes* he claims that a well-placed Watertown lawyer said, "Had [Gordie] been an out-of-town boy practicing here, he would have got off with a slap on the wrist," and then he adds the note toward which, in his mind, the entire affair had pointed: ". . . it had suddenly occurred to me that my home town would have disbarred me from something if it could, preferably the human race."

This lugubrious and self-pitying view of Watertown permeates Fred's work, yet a more objective judgment surely would be less harsh. Fred admitted as much to Paul Hemphill in 1976, when he said, "You Southerners like to talk about roots, like you invented it, but I got news for *y'all*. Everybody wants to go back home." Certainly Fred Exley did. He went back home over and over again, and not just because home is where they have to take you in. Watertown and the surrounding countryside were the only world in which he was entirely comfortable, a place he knew intimately, where he was known and where his many eccentricities were, for whatever inexplicable reason, not merely tolerated but subsidized.

The truth is that whatever inner wounds it may have inflicted upon him, Watertown in Fred's youth was a good place to be. It had a sense of communal identity that bred self-confidence as well as insularity. In northern New York State it was the center of the universe. Its plants made products that people needed, its football teams stood up to the best that Albany and Syracuse could field, its girls were the prettiest and its guys were the most loyal. The important places in Fred's life were the Public Square in the heart of town, ringed by the shops and offices to which people came from all around; the YMCA, just off the square, where teenagers crowded happily after school and on weekends; the Crystal Restaurant, where Leo Dephtereos's father served excellent food at bargain-basement prices; the Strand, the Olympic, the Avon and the Palace, where films brought in the outside world; Watertown High School, where Fred's first romance flowered; even the Black River Valley Club, the haute-Wasp sanctuary Fred so bitterly denounced.

If Fred had been as unhappy there as he often claimed to have been, why is it that the friends of his Watertown boyhood were the only enduring friends of his entire life? When he went to New York City, as he occasionally did after his first book gave him a small place in its literary life, he often took a Watertown friend with him, not just for company—or free transportation—but as a reminder of the down-home qualities that were of central importance to him. When he went to Florida, he hung out with Gordie

Phillips. When he went to Hawaii, he accepted the patient hospitality of another Watertown friend, Jo Cole. No matter where he happened to be, what he talked about was Watertown; he called it Aguatown, and he regaled barflies from coast to coast with stories about its people and places, stories that he told over and over again because he could never hear them often enough. Anytime he went anywhere, sooner or later he packed up and went back home. In the emphatic words of Gordie Phillips, *"Everything goes back to Watertown."*

Watertown was the place, Earl Exley was the person. He must be approached with a degree of caution, for he was both Fred's father and the central character—apart from Fred himself—in the book that is Fred's literary legacy. The real Earl Exley and the Earl Exley who served Fred's literary purposes may not be, probably are not, exactly the same person. Just as we must be wary of writers lamenting the hometowns to which they allegedly cannot go back, so must we be on guard when sons write about fathers; for it is the son, not the father, who is usually the real business at hand, and the father is often recast to suit the son's convenience.

That having been acknowledged, it remains that all evidence points to the essential truth of Fred's portrait of Earl Exley and his influence on his Fred's life. For reasons that will be discussed shortly, Charlotte Merkley Exley, Fred's mother, was probably the most important person in his life, but her effects on him were different from Earl's. Charlotte encouraged Fred in many of the habits that were to afflict him (and thus all who knew him) during his life: his selfishness, his dependency, his irresponsibility, his sense of entitlement, his self-absorption. She did this because she loved him too much. Earl, by contrast, seems not to have loved him enough, or not to have known how to show whatever love it was that he did feel. The result was that his son came to adulthood with an emptiness at his core, "a longing in my heart":

> I suffered myself the singular notion that fame was an heirloom passed on from my father. Dead at forty, which never obviates the stuff of myths, my father acquired over the years a nostalgic eminence in Watertown; and, like him, I wanted to have my name called back and bantered about in consecrated whispers. Perhaps unfairly to him (I have his scrapbooks and know what enviable feats are inventoried there), I'm not sure my father's legend was as attributable to his athletic prowess as to his personality. The tales men selected to pass on about him were never so much about a ninety-yard run as about an authentically colorful man having a ball and in an amiable way thumbing his nose at life.

His father's early death was a heavy weight for Fred to bear. Years later he told an interviewer, "I was sure I was going to die at forty. That was one of the worst years for me. My father was so athletic, and so virile and masculine. . . . I must have been carrying around all these years the notion that nobody was going to outlive my old man. When, in fact, my family is known for its longevity on both sides."

Earl Exley was born on January 14, 1905, in Malone, a small town about a hundred miles northeast of Watertown and ten miles south of the Canadian border. Of his ancestry, nothing is known except that the blood was predominantly Scots-English and that his parents had entered the country from Canada; ancestry has never been of interest to the

Exley family and no records of it have been kept. In this they are characteristically American, looking to the present and the future rather than to the past. We do know, though, that Earl's parents, William and Isabelle, were poor. When they moved to Watertown during Earl's boyhood, they took up residence in a neighborhood called the Oriental Flats, which was hardly better than a slum. As a schoolboy at the Hamilton Street School, Earl had only one shirt, which his mother washed each night and ironed the next morning.

This self-sacrificing devotion was rewarded. Earl was a decent if not brilliant student, and a superb athlete. At Watertown High School he starred in football, basketball and baseball, the first of these most particularly. He stood only five feet ten inches and weighed, in school, only about one hundred and sixty-five pounds, but he was strong, coordinated and determined. For Watertown, high school football was of indescribable importance, as it was for many other American towns and small cities seeking to prove themselves to the larger world. The high school team represented not merely the school and its students but the town and its citizens. How the team fared was a question of intense interest; players who advanced its fortunes in especially dramatic ways became local idols as teenagers and retained that exalted status for the rest of their lives, no matter what disappointments or failures awaited them in adulthood. Their days in the sun lasted forever, and nothing that followed glowed so brightly.

Earl Exley was the brightest of them all. He played fullback or halfback on offense, backfield on defense. In a tough game against Oneida "the human battering ram," as the *Watertown Daily Times* called him, kept his team from what could have been an embarrassing loss to a lesser rival by grinding out "a series of line bucks," and on defense "intercepted an Oneida pass and ran 15 yards before he was downed." Early in his career, in a loss to St. John's, he "was by far the hero for the locals and in fact was the only one who showed promise of developing into a real star of the gridiron." In a win over Cazenovia he played so hard that he "collapsed as the team was leaving the field and was unconscious for some time in a state of nervous exhaustion." Against Syracuse, an opposing player "resented Exley's ability to stop runner after runner," and expressed that resentment by approaching "the husky Purple and White star as he was resting on his hands and knees and [kicking] him in the neck." Football in Earl's time was a rough game, as the *Daily Times* noted when *A Fan's Notes* was published:

> In those days when he was playing football on the high-school team it was not mandatory to wear a helmet, and when the going got rough on the gridiron and yards were needed, Exley would yank off his helmet and put down his head, while carrying the ball, and ram into opposition players.
>
> He played in an era when football players were two-[way] performers. There was no offensive or defensive squad. He not only could carry the ball, but was fearless on defense and was considered a hard, deadly tackle.

By his senior year, 1924–25, Earl's place in the firmament was assured. He was, according to the *Daily Times,* "the greatest fullback that had ever been developed at the Watertown High School," "the hardest hitting back that ever plunged into a Watertown enemy's line and his tackling has always been sure and deadly," and: "Besides shining on the football field, basketball court and baseball diamond Exley has been a model student. During the past year he has seldom fallen below 80 per cent in a subject and as Gary M. Jones, principal of the school, said recently, 'Exley has asked no favors of anyone and has set a good example for every student.' "

This was not hyperbole. Earl Exley came as advertised. He was modest, humble and friendly. In his photograph in the 1925 Annual, he smiles up at the camera from under a shock of hair parted exactly in the middle, his smile confident but not cocky, his face beefy but pleasant. He was chosen "Best Sport," "Most Athletic" and "Hardest to Rattle," while the class prophecy had him "coaching football at Syracuse," and his verse read:

> *His athletic ability cannot be excelled;*
> *As a student he's one of the best.*
> *He is witty and wise and his limit is the skies*
> *And we know he will be a success.*

It didn't work out that way. College, which even ordinary athletes now take for granted, was an unlikely option for most Watertown youths in the mid-twenties unless they happened to come from the Four Hundred. In the summer of 1924 Earl had been spirited away by athletic supporters of Hobart College in Geneva, a hundred miles to the southwest. He actually went there and trained with the team, but the same Gary M. Jones who so admired his "good example" pointed out to Hobart that the youth had not finished his required high school work, so back to Watertown he went.

In his senior year he completed his academic obligations and led the football team to one of the most rewarding seasons in the school's history: eleven victories, one by the score of 119–0, and no losses. Most important, Charlotte Merkley, a member of the junior class, came into his life. "During his senior year my father had fallen in love with my mother and had determined to marry her at the expense of either education or fame."

This Earl Exley did with panache. On Wednesday, November 25, 1925, a dance was held at Watertown High School. Earl and Charlotte were there. When an intermission was announced, they left the dance hall quietly and went to St. Paul's Church, where they were married by its rector. Then they went back to the dance, where Earl's best man "tipped off the orchestra leader," according to the *Daily Times,* "and the orchestra broke into the strains of the wedding march." Congratulations were offered all around, and their life together began.

It did so without benefit of honeymoon. Where Earl and Charlotte spent their wedding night is not recorded, but the next afternoon—Thursday, Thanksgiving Day—he was committed to playing for the town's semiprofessional football team, the Red and Black. The game was called when only four of the Syracuse players showed up, but two days later Syracuse was ready. The game was played in bitter cold on an icy field. The Red and Black won, 9–0, and Earl, playing right halfback, made a thirty-yard gain on a pass play.

Earl and Charlotte set up housekeeping at 117 Washington Street, one of Watertown's principal thoroughfares. There they began a family that eventually included four children: Bill, Fred and his twin sister, Frances, and Connie. Earl worked for the telephone company as a lineman, making eleven dollars a week; the next year he was employed in the same capacity by the Central New York Power Corporation, where he remained until 1943, when he developed lung cancer. Work was necessary but peripheral to his life. He had been a football star in high school and he remained one, in actuality as well as in reputation, for much of the rest of his life. He played so well for the Red and Black that for a time after his retirement from the game a most-valuable-player award was given in his name. Crowds in the thousands came out for Red and Black games, paying admission prices that the players divided up—three or four dollars apiece is what it usually came to—as reward for their labors. Big-city professional football was young and little noticed, and "town ball" was the most likely outlet for an adult's athletic skills and energies; the money helped, but it was the joy of playing as well as, perhaps, the perpetuation and enhancement of the Exley legend that kept Earl in the game. "My father . . . took his pleasure in the grim Sunday afternoon world of semiprofessional athletes seeking violently to recapture a sense of a talent that may never have existed."

Earl loved his wife and their children, but in his fashion. The local habit of alcoholism had not gone unacknowledged in his family—both of his brothers died of it—and Earl was a ready, eager conscript. Like every man in working-class Watertown who liked a drink, Earl took his medicine in bars rather than at home. The nights he came home drunk were the ones when he and Charlotte were most apt to argue. The children could hear their harsh words through the thin walls of their little house at 393 Moffett Street and dreaded them, but Earl seems to have used words rather than his fists. There is no evidence either that he beat his wife—a most common practice among men of his time and class, and one that his younger son would adopt—or that he spanked his children.

He was, in fact, at a certain level a gentle soul. There had been no books in the house in which he grew up, and there were relatively few in his own, but he was sensitive and had interests larger and more complex than his athletic celebrity would suggest. He kept a scrapbook that provides a small window into his inner self. Some of what he pasted into it is predictable: clippings regarding a controversy over the Jefferson County Baseball League's "Umpires Union," of which Earl was an active member; photos of Babe Ruth and Lou Gehrig annotated with Earl's recollections of them; headlines announcing the deaths of presidents and kings, or natural and man-made disasters. Yet there are also articles about Beale Street in Memphis, "Where the Blues Began"; about the mystery of sleep; about the "trickery" of crystal-gazing; about the drowning of four nuns in an auto crash. There are, further, two saccharine poems: "My Baby's Birthday" and "The Lineman," the latter a eulogy to Earl's line of work written by a practitioner of it.

Not merely did Earl read poetry, he wrote it. Unfortunately no examples have survived, but he carefully preserved a card from Buckingham Palace, dated January 13, 1943: "The Private Secretary is commanded by The King to acknowledge the receipt of Mr. Earl E. Exley's letter of the 30th November with the accompanying copy of his poem 'This Time Canada, This Time', for which the Private Secretary is desired to express His Majesty's thanks." Though his education was limited, he was, his son thought, "a man of mercurial intelligence," and he looked at the world with curious, sympathetic eyes.

At least from time to time, Earl enjoyed the company of his wife and children; if he was playing in or umpiring a game, the whole family accompanied him and watched from the sidelines. The world of men rather than that of women and children was his true métier, but he tried to be a good father. He teased the children in a friendly way and could make Charlotte laugh when she was upset. He liked to tell stories and did so engagingly. He built a little cottage by Lake Ontario, on land leased from a church, and took the family there in the summer; the house had only one room, and the boys—Fred and Bill—slept in a loft.

How Fred felt about his father at the time—as opposed to how he felt as an adult, not to mention as a writer using his father for thematic purposes—is not entirely clear. The question too often asked of him—"Earl Exley your father?"— was tiresome and irritating, and he once said in exasperation, "If every son of a bitch in Watertown who told me he played with Earl actually had, they'd have had thousand-man football teams." Being the son of the local football hero could be a pain. But there can be little doubt that Fred's father aroused more pride than envy in him, that being the son of the famous "Ex" was itself no small distinction.

On one occasion, though, it was a terrible, unbearable burden. The account of that event as presented in *A Fan's Notes* is true. At thirteen Fred was a freshman in high school and a substitute on the junior-varsity basketball team. One evening his team played an exhibition against a pickup team of adults, one of whom was Earl Exley. Fred was sick the night of the game, but Earl talked him into playing:

> Gently he asked me to get up, for him; to go through this one game, for him; telling me that if I did this one thing, for him, he'd permit me to quit the team after the game. The gymnasium was packed, and the better part of the evening I sat on the bench stupefied, drifting between nausea and fear of having to go into the game. In an effort to humor the crowd, the coach ordered me in to guard my father in the

waning moments of the final quarter. Nearly thirty-nine then, sweating profusely and audibly huffing from years of Camel smoking, from the center of the court and to the jubilant hilarity of the crowd, my father sank three set shots, characterized for me by a deafening *swiiisssshhhhh* of ball through net, in the less than two minutes I covered him.

After the game we walked home to Moffett Street across Hamilton Street, which was a lonely street then and settled with very few houses. The cold was fierce, the moon was bright, and the snow uttered melancholy oaths beneath our boots. In penance my father had his gloveless hand resting affectionately on my shoulder. "I'm sorry about tonight," he said. "I was lucky." But we both knew that he hadn't been; and all the way home I had had to repress an urge to weep, to sob uncontrollably, and to shout at him my humiliation and my loathing. "Oh, Jesus, Pop! *Why? Why? Why?*"

This heartbreaking passage, among the finest writing Fred ever did, suggests that Earl humiliated his son because "he so needed The Crowd" and its applause. But Fred, a fan rather than a star, may not have understood the instinctive response of the superior athlete to competition. No doubt Earl knew full well that was his own son guarding him, but it may not have mattered. On the court, the ball in his hands, the crowd at full throat, he was urged by every instinct within him to put the ball into the air and to score.

That night was Earl Exley's last moment in the sun. "Neither of us knew . . . that in little over a year my father would be dead from the cancer which was doubtless even then eating away at him." Soon he was sent to the Ray Brook Sanatorium in Saranac Lake, where in the isolation of his room he accepted the ministrations of the doctors and nurses, and ruminated about his past and future. If he knew he was dying, he did not say so, but in a remarkable series of letters to Charlotte he attempted to atone for past errors, to reassure her of his love and to solicit her expressions of love for him.

The letters are written in pencil on cheap paper. None of them is dated and they contain no other evidence of chronology, so it is impossible to chart the rise and fall of Earl's moods. Medical news is infrequent: "I have been terribly sick again. My heart started acting up again last Tuesday and they had to start giving me Digitallus again. My stomach has been upset and I have had the diarraha." Or, "There is not much news only that I have to have another operation on my neck." There are reports on the weather and the books he is reading, requests for packages from home, reflections upon the kindness of his fellow workers at the power company.

Mostly, though, these letters are plaintive words from a man who knew that, in ways that cannot be measured on the playing field, he had fallen short. "Please don't forget that whatever I ever did in the past I've always loved you only." "My love for you seems to increase daily and I am earnestly looking for the day when I can really hold you in my arms and make up for some of the sad times I caused you in the past." "I love all the children but probably have had a funny way of showing it. I always admired everything they did and was always so proud of them all. They were such lovely babies and such fine youngsters that it wouldn't have been much of a man that did not love and respect such a fine family as I have." And, most poignant of all:

I have nearly got in 19 of the most happy years of my life. If you could only realize what it has meant to me to be married to you you could feel very proud and the grand family we have raised all tends to make me fight all the harder to get back on my feet so that we can be together again soon. Memories are so comforting to me here that I just can't help my eyes from filling up and have to swallow my heart three or four times.

While Earl was at Ray Brook some of his friends in Watertown decided to hold an all-star basketball game to raise funds for his medical expenses and for his family's support. The game was played on the night of January 1, 1945, between a Rotary team and a team of Old-Timers, who won by a score of 30–28. The weather was dreadful, but six hundred people were in the stands and about one thousand dollars was raised. Several days later Earl wrote a letter to the *Daily Times*. He said: "There is one spot in Watertown where the fineness of the night will never die—the Exley household. For me or for any of mine to forget this noble gesture would be a sacrilege in its basest form. To have had this honor even without the money angle, is something that can come only once in a man's life span. It is an unforgettable climax to 25 years of athletic play and interest."

"A sacrilege in its basest form": Did Earl know as he wrote those words that Fred had declined to attend the game? He had "refused utterly to sit red-facedly in that packed gymnasium and allow people to beam their beneficence down upon me." Partly out of pride, partly out of shame, this fifteen-year-old boy had "apprehensively hidden in a movie theater while [the game] was being played," unable to face "the humiliation of charity." This can surprise no one who remembers what it is like to be fifteen years old, but if Earl knew of Fred's one-boy boycott, he must have been embarrassed and puzzled. To a man who had played to the crowd all his life, his son's refusal to sit in that crowd must have seemed willfully perverse, and that phrase in Earl's letter may have been intended as a rebuke. Whatever the case, in this quiet rebellion Fred had laid the groundwork for themes he would explore twenty years later in a book of unsparing self-discovery.

Not long after the basketball game, Charlotte "finally brought my father home from Ray Brook at Saranac Lake to die." She put him in the Jefferson County Sanatorium, "a lovely hospital with sweeping, tree-shaded lawns at the top of Coffeen Street hill in Watertown." Fred and his twin sister, Frances, being "at an age too 'tender' to witness the horror of lingering death, . . . were packed off to a sympathetic and generous aunt in Westchester," where they continued their education at a local school. But Fred was back in Watertown that summer, and was at football practice on the morning of August 7, 1945, when he was approached by the town's renowned coach, William Graf. "Your father is dead," he told Fred, and then announced the news to the team. Earl Exley was gone, but for his son there remained nearly half a century of wrestling with his ghost.

FREDERICK EARL EXLEY, BORN MARCH 28, 1929, WAS A
wonder child. Charlotte's pregnancy had been unremarkable, so when, on that date, she gave birth to a daughter, she
assumed that her day's labors were complete. But thirty
minutes later she produced a second child, a son. Though
contemporary readers may regard any "miraculous" aspects
of this primarily as commentaries on the state of obstetrics
in Watertown in 1929, the baby's mother clearly saw it as
something more: Fred—the name had no family connotations and was chosen merely because Charlotte and Earl
liked it—was a gift to her, and she treated him as such for
the rest of her life.

Not merely was he a gift, he was an uncommonly precious one who could be taken away at any moment. The
infant boy who emerged from Charlotte's womb was not
breathing, and for a few moments his survival was in question. The doctors brought him around, but Charlotte never
forgot the circumstances of his arrival. Early on little Fred-

die learned that if he held his breath, he could get Charlotte to do whatever he wanted. This set a pattern that never thereafter varied: Fred demanded and Charlotte granted. Her gratitude for having him was matched by her sense of his fragility and vulnerability. She assumed that he needed more protection from life's vagaries than is afforded to most of us, and she made certain that he got it.

Given the sort of person she was, this is not surprising. Almost all the people who knew Fred Exley knew his mother as well. Among them were seasoned, skeptical men and women from Watertown and Alexandria Bay, writers and editors and other cynics from New York City; not once did any of them, talking about the ups and downs of their relationships with this exasperating man, say a single harsh word about Charlotte Merkley Exley. Everyone remarked upon her bottomless kindness and generosity, her eagerness to please, her unwavering good humor, the bountiful table she set.

Like Earl Exley's, Charlotte's family had entered the United States from Canada, in their case illegally. Slightly more is known about her background than Earl's. Her grandmother, Fanny Champ, née Maguire, "worked as a cook and a domestic at the Frontenac Hotel" in the Thousand Islands of the St. Lawrence; it is from her that the Irish strain flowed into Fred's blood and with it "drunkenness, garrulousness, wit, deviousness, scatology, humor, mysticism, blarney, amorality, poverty, xenophobia, blasphemy, reverence for language and tale-telling." She married, was widowed, and married again. This second union was with John Champ, a native Englishman who had come to the United States after fighting for his old country in the ghastly battle at Balaklava in the Crimean War; he soon found himself fighting for his new country, for the Union army as a member of an upstate New York artillery company. After the war he and Fanny settled in Watertown, where "he became a kind of ne'er-do-well 'country squire' with a silver-handled walking stick, an incredibly handsome man with a magnificent mane of snow-white hair and a great gray beard, and lived out his life with his memories of blood and thunder, carnage and cannon, and died in his sleep at his Massey Street home . . . in 1909, at age 77."

One of their two children, Nellie, married Henry Merkley. Their life was not easy. They had three children: two daughters—Charlotte, born at Massena on March 30, 1906, and her older sister, Frances—and a son, who died as a youngster, probably from cystic fibrosis, a disease that reappeared in the family two generations later. Nellie went deaf from scarlet fever when Charlotte was a girl, forcing both girls to take on heavy responsibilities and, it seems safe to assume, establishing in Charlotte the habit of self-sacrifice.

Charlotte was of average height with a large build; after four children and two husbands she gained a substantial amount of weight and became a perpetual, albeit unsuccessful, dieter, but those who knew her when she was young remember her as lovely, a good and fitting catch for the football hero. Probably she made him happier than he made her. Certainly that is the most likely inference to be drawn from the letters quoted in the previous chapter, an impression that is reinforced by her readiness to remarry after Earl's death.

But if she felt any disappointments or harbored any resentments about her marriage, she did not permit them to color her child-rearing responsibilities. In these she was unfailingly faithful. With Earl only an intermittent presence in the household, Charlotte was in charge. Fred liked to characterize his family as "rowdy, impoverished, argumentative, disorderly," but a more revealing and accurate insight is that "ours is a family whose various doors are by tacit agreement left open to one another." Charlotte bound the family together not by force but by love and a tolerance for the distinctive qualities of each of its members. "An innocent who had for so many years kept her mind unsullied by evil," she "believed in wholesome food, clean clothes, and warm beds for her family."

Charlotte's hopes for Fred were conventional; she wanted him to get a secure job, marry and have a family. Fred thwarted her at every turn, yet she rolled with every punch and catered to his every whim. In response he rarely drank or used foul language in her presence, but otherwise the relationship between them was played by his rules. She kept extra cartons of cigarettes in her house, terrified that he might drop by and his own supply suddenly run out. If he was on the wagon, as from time to time he was, she resisted making demands on him because "I don't want to upset him, he might start drinking again." She waited on him hand and foot, and if his friends were in town, she waited on them as well. Mel Zerman, who was in the sales department at Harper & Row when *A Fan's Notes* was published, stopped by with his wife in the summer of 1973. They'd been on the road for a while and had a carload of laundry. Not merely did Charlotte insist on washing it, she ironed it as well. Later Bob Loomis came up from Random House for a visit. At dinner in her tiny house there were four of them: Bob, Fred, Charlotte and her dog, Killer. But the table was piled high enough to feed fifty people, with meat and vegetables and at least five kinds of potatoes.

Charlotte believed in love, but not in tough love. If Fred was lazy or dependent or self-absorbed, nothing that Charlotte did diminished these characteristics in any way. If he was a baby all his life, as he was, much of the responsibility must be laid upon her. Inasmuch as his state of perpetually arrested infancy was as much a part of him as his drinking, it must be accepted as part of what made him the writer he was. But as a man it left him incomplete. This was noticed in the late 1960s by Alice Denham, a first novelist and Greenwich Village habitué who enjoyed, if that is the word for it, an intermittent affair with him for several years. During their first meeting she was surprised to learn, as she says in her memoir in progress, that he lived with his mother. "Mr. Macho with Mom?" she asked. "We get along," he replied. "Better than a wife." A few hours later they ended up in bed, an event she describes in clinical detail. The oedipal aspects of this vignette should not be overplayed, but they do tend to jump off the page:

> "Why don't you get on the bed?" I invited.
> "This is how I like to do it." On his knees by my bed, going down on me.
> My scarlet ribbon stretched out and enjoyed it. Freddie was quite avid at this. Suddenly his bulbous blue eyes got baby big and he whimpered.
> "Does Mommy like her little boy?"
> "What?"
> "Is Mommy pleased?" His lips got pouty.
> "Oh, yes," I said. "Mommy likes it fine and dandy."

Of the three other children whom Charlotte raised, all managed to make productive lives for themselves in the conventional world. Her first, William Richard Exley, was born September 18, 1926. As a boy he was polite, reserved, intelligent, self-sufficient. He and Earl were close, and he made a mark in the Watertown public schools just as Earl had, though in his case it was more in academics than in athletics. This was double trouble for Fred, since coaches compared him with Earl and teachers compared him with Bill. When Fred began high school geometry class, the teacher asked whether he was Bill's brother. Yes, Fred said, whereupon the teacher told him that if he wasn't prepared to do as well as Bill had, he wanted Fred to leave. Fred walked out.

Bill was born to be a soldier. As a boy he played with guns and tin soldiers, and as soon as he got out of high school he entered the navy. His rise was hampered by his lack of a college degree, much less one from the Naval Academy, but when he moved over to the army after World War II he made steady progress. His field was intelligence; he was carrying out his duties as a forward observer in Korea when a land mine destroyed his jeep and seriously wounded him. Once he recovered he began a series of assignments that took him to Berlin, to Baltimore, to the Pentagon, to Hawaii and then to Vietnam in the late 1960s. By then he had a wife, Judy, herself an army brat, and a son, Scot, with whom he enjoyed making lead soldiers and dioramas of battles. Like his brother, Bill was a heavy drinker who consumed vast quantities of beer and whose car was often littered with empties, but unlike his brother he held it well and apparently did not permit it to interfere with his work.

Eventually Bill rose to the rank of colonel. He took many secrets to his grave when he died of cancer, at age forty-six. He never spoke to his wife about his intelligence missions, and he certainly never spoke about them to his younger brother, who liked to fantasize that Bill had a "license to kill" and that his activities were authorized by the highest authorities. This made provocative raw material for Fred's third book, *Last Notes from Home,* but its connection to reality is at best unclear. What mattered most about Bill to Fred was that he embodied a life Fred knew he was incapable of leading himself, a life contained within the limits of work and marriage and white picket fences and the dutiful assumption of responsibilities that are not always welcome.

Charlotte's second child, Frances, Fred's twin, was closest in nature and character to her mother. If being a twin was important to Fred, he gave little sign of it. To Frances, though, it was as much a gift as Fred himself had been to their mother. She adored being a twin, and she adored her brother; she was "one of those grotesquely irritating people born utterly free of envy, malice or the capacity to ridicule." As a child she did everything for Fred, including covering up for his misbehavior; when in a prank he shot her with a blank cartridge, scaring her and Charlotte to death, she remained "as incapable of vengeance as any of the other base impulses" and cried out to an infuriated Earl, "Don't hurt him, Dad. *Please don't hurt him.* He was only kidding."

In school the twins were at first inseparable, but gradually began to go in their own directions as Fred was steered into shop class and Fran into homemaking. School, like society, was moving them into conventional male and female roles. Fred hung out with the jocks and the hellraisers, seemingly indifferent to the good opinion of his schoolmates. Fran, on the other hand, dearly wanted to be popular and was given what she desired. Everyone loved her. She was tall, pretty, eager to please. She was head cheerleader and was voted most popular in her class. She had two steady boyfriends, first Fred's friend and fellow athlete

Mike Bresnahan, then Bill Graf, the son of the football coach.

After high school Fran trained as a medical technologist, learning clinical laboratory procedures, and worked for eight years at a hospital outside New York City, near her beloved aunt and namesake, Frances Knapp. In Mount Vernon she met and soon married Irwin Brown, who ran a record store there until Sam Goody and other big discount operations put him out of business. In the mid-1950s they moved to Watertown, where Irwin got a job as a social worker before entering what became a long, successful career in public education, culminating in his appointment as principal of Indian River Central School. He and Fran had four children, but her domestic chores did not prevent her from resuming her laboratory work. Both Fran and Irwin became prominent, respected and admired members of the upstate community; Fran in particular was known and loved for unstinting, large-hearted public service. They bought a house at Cape Vincent on Lake Ontario, then a small compound of houses at Washington Island, outside Clayton in the St. Lawrence. It was to an A-frame in the latter that Fred repaired in order to write his last book and to take advantage of Fran's desire to please him.

Notwithstanding the innumerable goods and services Fran provided for him, Fred could be gratuitously cruel to her. If she happened to wander into an Alexandria Bay bar at which he was holding forth, and to say to those accompanying her, "This is my brother," he would walk away from her, apparently because he—he who at times looked the perfect slob—took fastidious offense at the substantial weight she, like their mother, had gained over the years. He called her Big Mama, which seems to have arisen from affection tempered by derision.

The last of Charlotte's four children, Constance, was born August 13, 1933. She was a typical youngest child, catered to a little more than the others, most particularly by her father, whom she accompanied on early-morning fishing trips and other excursions. Like her mother and sister she was large-boned, but managed to remain sturdy rather than heavy. In high school she met John O'Neill, himself as solid and purposeful as she, and married him not long after her graduation in 1951. John worked for a while for a paper company, and for a couple of years they lived in Florida while he held a construction job, but after the mid-fifties his principal employment was with the telephone company, as a cable splicer and technician. He became expert on telephone service to the Thousand Islands in the St. Lawrence River, and over the years acquired a knowledge of the river that bordered on encyclopedic. For a while Connie worked in a doctor's office, but as their family grew she concentrated on her life at home, not merely because she felt this to be her proper duty but because their eldest son had cystic fibrosis and required more attention than most children.

Connie and John provided an antidote to the unquestioning self-abnegation that Charlotte and Fran accorded to Fred. Like Bill, Connie had decided that the healthiest response to the somewhat overheated emotional climate that Fred created within the Exley household was distance. Where Fran would eagerly grant whatever Fred requested or demanded, Connie met each entreaty with skepticism; she would provide what was genuinely needed, or what Fred simply could not do for himself, but she had no interest in being his handmaiden. She agreed with Bill, who used to say, "I've got a family of my own. We've all got our problems. I don't tell you about mine, don't tell me about yours." This was easier for Bill to bring off than it was for her, since he was far away and she had chosen to remain in the bosom of her family. It helped that she had John, who was devoted to everyone in the family except Fred, with whom he had an uneasy relationship, in large measure because he thought Fred was lazy; he adamantly refused to do Fred's bidding and called him to account when his selfishness made undue demands on Connie or other family members. Yet there was a certain respect between the two men. John found Fred interesting and intelligent, and Fred saw in John the same quality he saw in Bill.

"I really don't know how you do it," Fred once said to John. "I mean, get up every morning, go punch a time clock."

John replied somewhat testily, "I don't punch a time clock."

"Yeah," Fred said, "but you're *there* every day. Myself, I couldn't do it."

So now the curtains part and Frederick Earl Exley moves into the only place he ever wanted to be: the limelight, the starring role, the absolute and unchallenged center of attention. What a piece of work he was! Contradiction was, or should have been, his middle name. He felt that the world owed him a living, yet money meant little to him. He sponged off everyone who entered his life, yet he could be unexpectedly and unaffectedly generous. His judgments of others could be merciless—there was scarcely a soul in his life against whom he did not turn at one time or another—

yet his loyalty was ferocious. He sought the respect and the company of the literary elite, yet he was egalitarian to the bone. He was a great big baby who never grew up, yet he better than anyone else knew his shortcomings and failures.

He was a singular man. The rules the rest of us live by simply didn't apply to him; not merely did he believe this, but somehow he conned everyone else into believing it as well. He had a quality that Irwin Brown deftly summarized in a single word: *Fredness.* The whole extended Exley family might be assembled around Charlotte's or Fran's or Connie's table for Thanksgiving dinner. Was Fred coming? Who knew? Suddenly there he was. He ate a few bites, then hit the road. "Well, I have to go. Bye." What did the family say? "That's Freddie."

There's a Fred Exley story about his being in the apartment of a moderately well-known New York journalist, a woman with whom he had a slight friendship. She vanished for about forty-five minutes. "What's going on?" he called out. "Where are you?" A door opened and the woman came back into the room. She knelt on the floor before Fred's chair, unzipped his fly and gave him a blow job. Is the story true or is it fiction? Nobody knows except the two people in that room, both of whom are dead, but the person to whom Fred told the story laughed and said, "It's a *strange* story. It's just another Fred story, let's put it that way: Believe it or not. The guy was just endlessly interesting."

His selfishness, his sense of entitlement, was stupendous: outrageous and infuriating, yet hilarious and endearing. No one upon whom he made demands—and he made demands on everyone—stayed angry at him for long. Around 1953 he showed up, unannounced, at Fran and Irwin's door in Westchester. These were hard times for them, but as soon as he crossed the threshold he asked, "Can I stay here for a while?" It was all she could do to feed her husband and young family, but Fran immediately picked up old habits and began waiting on him.

"Get me a sandwich!"

"What kind do you want?"

"Oh, what you got?"

"Tuna fish, salami."

"I'll take tuna fish."

For week after week he sat in the middle of his bed, in his underwear, wrapped in blankets, ordering Frances this way and that. Then just like that—poof!—he was gone. Fran was hurt and Irwin was annoyed, but there was always the explanation: "Oh, that's Freddie."

This is the tolerant view of Fred's utter self-absorption, his assumption that not merely did the world owe him a living, it was expected to pay up voluntarily and without complaint. The harsh view is that he was a user, a professional guest, though this begs the question of what exactly it was about him that exacted favors from people, favors that, if requested by most of us, would be refused without a second thought. During the first couple of weeks that he knew Gordon Phillips, Fred borrowed (and never repaid) two dollars. This set a pattern that persisted throughout a half century of friendship, to the extent that over the years Fred was into Phillips for something on the order of twenty thousand dollars. It was money Fred expected and never questioned; not merely that, he took genuine offense if any conditions were attached to these subsidies.

Once Gordie was in Florida, alone, when Fred called and said he wanted to join him.

"Fine, Freddie, come on down."

"Well, I need a ticket."

"All right, I'll get you a ticket. How about ten days?"

"What do you mean, ten days? Aren't you going to be there for two months?"

"Yeah, I'm going to be down here for two months, but *you're* not. My daughter is coming down at spring break, and I've got some other commitments."

"Well, fuck you, you cheap son of a bitch. I'm not coming."

On another occasion Gordie was living and practicing law in Albany. Fred was married to his first wife, Francena, but was spending little time with her. He showed up one day at Gordie's for the weekend and stayed for months, lying around on the sofa all day, exchanging bits of conversation with Gordie's girlfriends, clients and other visitors, in a state of perpetual inebriation. One day he finally stirred.

"I gotta get laid," he said.

"Well, sober up," Gordie said, "and I can fix you up."

"I will, I will."

Gordie knew a couple of available women, one of whom he thought would like Fred. "Have I got a girl for you!" he said. "I'll make the connection." This he did, successfully. He knew Fred wouldn't telephone the woman, so he told her, "O'Connor's Restaurant, six o'clock, tomorrow night. I'll tell Fred what you look like." He reported all this to Fred, who said, "Great! Great!"

The appointed hour rolled around. As he was about to leave, Fred said to Gordie, "Hey, I gotta have some money." Gordie gave him twenty-five dollars. Fred went into orbit.

"You cheap son of a bitch!" he shouted. "You think I can take a girl out on twenty-five bucks?"

Gordie reached for his wallet. "Not to worry, Freddie. Here's a hundred dollars. Just make sure you save enough money to buy a bus ticket back to fuckin' Greenwich, because you're outta here."

Freddie went on his date, bought his bus ticket and went back to Francena.

Once Fred became famous, or semifamous, he extended his universe of entitlement to book publishing and journalism. His correspondence with Jann Wenner, of *Rolling Stone,* is riddled with demands for money, or airline tickets, or hotel reservations. In August 1986 he wrote a letter to Bob Loomis that deserves to be quoted at length, for it is quintessential Exley:

> Presently I'm planning on taking you . . . up on your invitation to be Random House's guest for a few days in NYC. I thought I'd come Saturday, September 27, see the Giants-Saints game Sunday, then spend Monday and Tuesday morning with you going over the manuscript. This will entail a hotel reservation from Saturday night September 27 through Monday night, September 29. This is the part that everyone but Jann Wenner seems to have difficulty understanding. Unless one has a credit card, which I don't, the hotel expects you to pay cash in advance. For that reason, Wenner gives the hotel his corporate credit card number and in return gets a letter from the reservations manager stating that that number will be honored. He then sends a xerox of the letter to me, and in case the guy isn't in the hotel on my arrival I can present his letter to the desk clerk. In that way I don't immediately get hit for three fucking days lodging, get put on cash and carry for my morning coffee and eggs and so forth. Even the New York Times didn't understand this. Although they put up all kinds of guys at

the hotel where . . . I stayed, they didn't seem to understand those guests guarantee the Times's paying by giving them a credit card of their own. That is, if the Times doesn't pay, the guy has guaranteed payment with his own card. Explaining this over and over again makes me view the world as simpleminded, and I can honestly—no shit!—feel my blood pressure skyrocketing.

It takes no great leap of the imagination to see Fred at his typewriter, his patience exhausted by the sheer simplemindedness of the rest of humanity, thinking through this elaborate scheme for the subsidy of his royal highness—Irwin Brown liked to call him The King—and then spelling it all out for the dimwit at the receiving end of that letter. Yet this was the same Fred Exley who, while visiting Loomis in Sag Harbor, became worried about the safety of the household's shower stall. So he lurched off to a hardware store and purchased grit for its floor. He was afraid someone was going to slip and fall.

Asked what they found about Fred that was likable, or endearing, or what it was that Fred gave them in exchange for the many demands he so routinely made, his friends used certain words repeatedly as well as independently of one another: loyalty, generosity, kindness, sweetness, integrity, goodness, gentleness. They talked about his utter lack of pretension, his ease with people of all stations and occupations. David Hirshey was a young editor at the New York *Daily News* when he and a friend met Fred and then accompanied him to a bar in Manhattan. Later, as an editor at *Esquire,* Hirshey became important to Fred, but at the time he was just another journalist while Fred, as the author of *A Fan's Notes,* was a mythical figure among Hirshey's crowd. Yet Fred spent six hours with Hirshey, who was left to wonder how many other well-known writers would have done the same.

But if Fred the adult was a creature of contradictions and of eccentricities bordering on the bizarre, what is doubly odd is that Fred the child and youth gave no hint of the Fred to come. He may not have been an ordinary child, but he gave a good impersonation of one. He was baby-faced—he was baby-faced throughout his life, which may have had something to do with the beard he began to affect in the 1970s—and outgoing. He was a show-off who liked to draw attention to himself, not always in the best of ways. In the second or third grade he took a poke at a teacher who caught him swinging from a pipe in the basement, an offense for which his father was summoned to school, but that was about as difficult as he ever got. He went to class, made decent grades, was confirmed in the Episcopal Church and otherwise behaved exactly as one would expect of a boy whose parents were rising, however uncertainly, into the middle class.

There was no reason to believe that any of this would change as Fred finished junior high and prepared to enter high school in the fall of 1943. He was a pleasant, unexceptional boy whom people liked but who made no deep or lasting impressions on anyone, a face in the crowd. That, as his remarkable book tells us, is what he expected to be for the rest of his life. But high school held surprises for him, not in the classroom or on the playing field, where his acceptable if generally unremarkable performance continued, but in three discrete events that altered him in ways about which we can only guess. One was the death of his father. The second was an auto accident in which he was seriously injured. The third was a brief romance that left him alienated and aware, perhaps for the first time, of the unbridgeable distance between him and everyone else. All three events combined to underscore his sense that he was somehow different from other people, to abet him in his instinct to follow his own inclinations and no one else's.

WATERTOWN HIGH SCHOOL WAS AN UNDISTINGUISHED three-story brick-and-stone building not far from the Square. It had fifteen hundred students, three grades in junior high and three in senior; though the junior and senior highs shared the same building, passage from the former to the latter was a major event that moved the student into a different world. For most students these last three years were the end of formal education. Even if they expected that the next stop was the power company or matrimony and motherhood, they took high school seriously and treasured the education and pleasures it offered.

The 1940s were a bright period in the school's history. Spirit was high, inflated if anything by wartime patriotism. The school—the classroom, the athletic fields and gymnasium, various extracurricular activities—was the center around which all else revolved. School life bore almost no resemblance to that of the late twentieth century. Students walked or rode bicycles; none owned cars, indeed the idea of

owning a car in the foreseeable future was beyond the imagination of all but the wealthiest, of whom there were not
many. Football games were important events that brought
the entire school together, from the pregame pep rallies with
bonfires and cheers to the postgame parties. Recreational
opportunities that school didn't offer were found at the
YMCA, where students played billiards and table tennis, or
read books and magazines in the big lobby with soft, comfortable chairs.

Dress was neat and manners were good. The teachers were
the law. They expected students to be quiet and attentive in
class; those who misbehaved were swiftly and emphatically
disciplined. There was a certain amount of cliquishness—
jocks hung out with jocks, the prettiest girls tended to flock
together—but students thought of themselves as part of a
larger whole of which they were proud, grateful members.
Language was clean; *damn* and *hell* were daring expletives,
the utterance of which would have landed a student in the
principal's office, while *fuck*—which Fred later used the way
most people use the definite article—was unimaginable
except, perhaps, behind the closed doors of the football locker
room.

Before school some students held what they called
"chapel," though its religious connotations were nonexistent. Boys and girls gathered in an auditorium, where they
talked quietly, perhaps kissed chastely. Boys tended to be
uncomfortable with girls, and vice versa. A kiss in chapel
was a big thing, and was often the end of the line. Even the
football players, to whom much was given, usually came as
virgins to graduation day, and girls clung tenaciously to
their virtue.

In this crowd of innocent young people, Fred moved quietly and unobtrusively. He had acquired his father's good looks and was a good dresser as well, but he was shy around girls. He played football and basketball, though with no great distinction, and he did little else. His classroom performance was satisfactory, but betrayed no hint of literary interests, nor is there any reason to believe that he did much reading beyond academic requirements. In contrast with Fran, who found time not merely to be head cheerleader but also to join the French Club, the Tri-Y, the yearbook staff, the student council and the Bowling Club, Fred had nothing to claim except sports, varsity and junior varsity. "We can't say enough about Fran—she's tops!" her yearbook said, but Fred was merely "Another great Exley," which cannot possibly have been the distinction he sought for himself.

But if Fred was not a star on the football or basketball team, his brief career as a high school athlete had a lasting effect on him, as did the manner in which it ended. Sports gave him a sense of male camaraderie that he replicated in later years in other places, most notably the bars he frequented throughout his life. It was not true of him, as it was of some of his friends, that his life stopped when football stopped, but his time on the gridiron was happy and he remembered it with affection. Football, he thought, "was an island of directness in a world of circumspection," to which he added:

In football a man was asked to do a difficult and brutal job, and he either did it or got out. There was nothing rhetorical or vague about it; I chose to believe that it was not unlike the jobs which all men, in some sunnier past, had been called upon to do. It smacked of something old, something traditional, something unclouded by legerdemain and subterfuge. It had that kind of power over me, drawing me back with the force of something known, scarcely remembered, elusive as integrity. . . .

For Fred and every other boy at Watertown High School, football was synonymous with William I. "Bill" Graf, "the coach who had produced the animals who had so impressed Paddy Brennon," the Haight-Ashbury saloonkeeper. Literally synonymous: in the sports pages of the *Watertown Daily Times,* the high school football teams were "Grafmen." Graf was "big, brawny, handsome, tawny-skinned, cigar-chomping, awe-inspiring." Fred compared him with Woody Hayes, the coach at Ohio State University in the postwar years who was celebrated, or despised, for a dogged ground game that eschewed the passing attack—and its risks—as well as for a right-wing political and cultural point of view. A more accurate comparison, though, is with Vince Lombardi, the coach of the Green Bay Packers professional team in the 1960s, who was famous, or notorious, for insisting that "victory is the only thing" and for inspiring a devotion among his players that often approached adoration.

Graf knew the raw material that had been given him: boys of narrow background and limited prospects who were boiling with unexpressed and inhibited urges. He believed that football offered a way to teach them to discipline themselves and to subordinate themselves to the group of which they were a part. Like many other coaches of the time he saw sports as a socializing influence as well as a form of exercise and competition. That view is no longer fashionable, but Graf's record suggests that there was real merit to it. A number of the boys who came to him from poor or struggling households learned under his tutelage how to be men, and went on to successful careers in medicine, the law and other mainstream middle-class endeavors. He taught them to believe in themselves.

There was nothing subtle about his methods. He was tough, and he expected his players to be tough. The annual game against Massena, a burly manufacturing town on the St. Lawrence, was always a particular challenge, and Graf knew how to get his team up for it. Once during Fred's time on the team Graf ordered all the players except the starters off the field, then looked at the first string and said, "You hit me, I'll hit you." Gene Renzi, the left guard, hesitated a moment, then gave the coach a tentative hit. Graf responded by whacking him full force. "He really nailed me," Renzi said half a century later. "I woke up. I would have killed my grandmother. He did it to all of us. We still talk about it. Today he'd be in jail. We *loved* it at that moment."

Fred remembered a day when, in practice, the right tackle missed a blocking assignment. "Graf whistled the scrimmage dead, nonchalantly walked to the right tackle, unsnapped and removed the right tackle's helmet. . . . Bill Graf raised his doubled fist high and with seemingly savage fury brought the heel of the fist smack down atop the right tackle's dome." In hindsight Fred suspected that Graf "pulled that punch," but the effect it had on the team was as desired; practice went on and on until the plays were run as Graf wanted them to be run, went on and on to the point of exhaustion and beyond. "That was one of the half-dozen nights during my football and basketball days under Bill

Graf when I put my head down on my folded arms on the kitchen table and fell into the stolid sleep of utter fatigue while my mother was rewarming my share of a supper eaten hours earlier by the family. So bad was it on this night she could not even rouse me until three a.m., when she again tried to feed me. But I waved the food away scornfully and barely struggled up the stairs and into bed, while the old lady in the housecoat stood at the bottom of the staircase and moved me on with a whispered hand-wringing litany of 'Dear, dear, dear, dear.' "

Graf wasn't merely a martinet; few coaches in any sport win year after year after year on the simple expedient of scaring their players into submission. Graf was also smart and well connected. He was friendly with Frank Leahy, the coach at Notre Dame whose record in thirteen years at that most famous of all football factories, from 1941 to 1953, was 107 victories, 13 losses and 9 ties. When Leahy came to power at Notre Dame the school's football reputation, exalted beyond imagination in the days of Knute Rockne, had sunk badly. Leahy restored it by jettisoning the old single-wing formation, which emphasized running, and replacing it with the T-formation, which placed primary responsibility on the quarterback and added passing and guile to the offensive repertoire. At a football camp in the Adirondacks in the summer of 1943, Leahy taught Graf the formation. "Thus for six, seven years, well into the 1950s for that matter, Watertown played against single- and double-wing-formation teams that hadn't the foggiest notion what we were doing on offense."

One of the strongest of those Watertown teams took the field in the fall of 1945, about a month after the death of Earl Exley. No one remembers that Fred grieved unduly for his father—indeed, no one remembers that Fred grieved at all, which is not surprising given his reticence about intimate personal matters—but it does not seem unreasonable to imagine that Earl was on his mind as the season began. Fred started at center on offense and at nose guard or linebacker on defense. Like his father, he was five feet ten inches tall and weighed about a hundred and sixty-five pounds. He compensated for his lack of size or innate skill by working diligently and with gusto, but he made one unfortunate mistake. "In our fourth game, at Auburn High School in gale-like winds and rains, I was called for holding on their one-yard line on fourth down. We scored, had the play nullified, were penalized 15 yards and on the replay from 16 yards out, we failed to put the ball in." Auburn won, 6–0. This was Watertown's only loss in eight games; it shut out six of those eight opponents and, overall, outscored them 157–12, a statistic that even Frank Leahy might have envied. Fred claimed in later years to have been haunted by this mistake, but he seems to have understood at the same time that more important matters than games were at stake:

Was it worth it all? To this day I don't honestly know. I do know that we won and won and won. I also know that to win and win and win leaves little time for anything else. I did not learn how to play a musical instrument or join the glee club. I never tried out for the school play. The thought of running for school office would have been absurd. After a Stetsoned cowboy I produced in kindergarten, I never did another watercolor. Even today my ignorance of music appalls me. Writing a speech for President Reagan would be beyond me. I could list the gaps in my education until the reader slumbered. One might very well ask, then, if being a jock cost me so dearly in other disciplines, why my feelings are in the least ambivalent.

There is nothing mysterious about that ambivalence. If, on the one hand, football circumscribed Fred's life, on the other it gave him things that he needed and valued. It connected him to his father, the importance of which should not be underestimated. While Earl was still alive his good opinion may well have meant more to Fred than anything on earth, and after his death Fred was left to puzzle out a relationship the precise nature of which had never been decided. On the football field or, later, in the stands or in a bar with the television set showing a game, Fred was in the company of his father. It was as simple as that.

It was also more than that. At the University of Southern California, which he entered in the fall of 1950, Fred discovered not merely the joys of spectator sport but their metaphoric and self-aggrandizing possibilities. It took him more than a decade to bring all of this into focus, but the vicarious connection he established with Southern Cal's glamorous running back, Frank Gifford, provided him with the central thematic device around which *A Fan's Notes* is constructed. When Gifford moved along to professional football and the New York Giants, Fred's public performance as a Giants' fan nonpareil came from the heart, but it was also essential to the Fred Exley mythology, the fabrication of which was among his chief labors in the long, arid years following the publication of *A Fan's Notes*.

Still, no one who knew Fred, especially those who knew him before a small measure of fame befell him, doubts that his ardor for the Giants was as intense as advertised. In front of the television set Fred was crazed. He yelled and screamed, leaped and collapsed. For a while he watched at Jasper's restaurant on the Square in Watertown, but he was so demonstrative that finally he was asked not to return. So he took his business to the New Parrot, a restaurant and bar to the south of town where the bartender, a friend, was more tolerant of his excesses.

Except during the early 1960s, when he lived with his mother and stepfather and occasionally watched a game at home with them, Fred always watched his football in a bar. This stands to reason, since he also preferred to do his drinking in bars, but there was a side benefit of which Fred was well aware. In a bar he was on public display, putting on a show. This drove some customers away, but "most of those who remained had seen the show before and had come back for more, bringing with them the morbid fascination which compels one to stare at a madman." In the years when his life seemed to be going nowhere, this gave him a certain local standing, if only as town lunatic-cum-alcoholic. Later, once Fred had published *A Fan's Notes,* he acquired a reputation as a football savant and parlayed it into a small, irregular cash flow. He twice wrote short pieces about football for *The New York Times;* for *The Cable Guide* he wrote about women and football, urging the former to follow the latter because of "the heroic strength, the strategic ingenuity, the collective artistry and masculine grace of a game that celebrates the worst and the best of the society of men"; for *Esquire* he revisited Southern Cal and the Rose Bowl; for *Inside Sports* he reminisced about Watertown and Coach Graf; and for *Rolling Stone* he wrote a long piece about professional football and drugs.

As a result of his obsession with football Fred also became the subject as well as the author of pieces about the game. Sports reporters looking for a quote often turned to him, and he was usually happy to oblige. *The Washington Post* twice published extensive pieces along the lines of "Notes on a Fan," and a magazine called *New York Sports* did one

called "A Giant Fan's Footnote." Perhaps the ultimate con-
firmation of Fred's rank as the nation's leading literary
football authority was extended by the American Library
Association, which in 1986 promoted the cause of reading
with a series of posters. One of these showed Dan Marino,
the brilliant quarterback of the Miami Dolphins, sitting in a
stadium, absorbed—or so we were expected to believe—in a
book. The book was *A Fan's Notes.*

The 1945 football season was the last Fred played. He probably wanted to continue the game in college, but any possibility of that was eliminated on the night of May 31, 1946.
Fred was standing outside the YMCA when Jean Hynes,
the sixteen-year-old daughter of a prominent local attorney,
drove by in her family's 1940 sedan. She stopped and asked
Fred if he would like to take a ride. He hopped in and off
they went, driving out of town to the south along the Watertown–Adams state highway. On a spot known locally as
Voodoo Hill, Jean apparently was blinded by the headlights
of an oncoming car. She lost control, went onto the soft
shoulder and then did a complete flop before landing right
side up. Jean was uninjured, but Fred, according to the
Daily Times, suffered "a fracture of the upper third of the
right humerus and injuries to the right elbow and ulnar
nerve resulting in an atrophy of the muscles of the right arm
and hand, and limitation of flexion of the right elbow, loss of
control and movement of the palmar surface and fingers of
the right hand."

The phone rang that night in the Exley house on Moffett
Street. Fran answered it. "You've got to come to the hospital
right away," she was told. "Your brother's been in an acci-

dent." Fred had to stay in the hospital for about six weeks. It is both puzzling and interesting that Fred, who squeezed just about every ounce of literary juice out of almost everything else in his life, made no use of this incident at all. Interesting and puzzling, that is, because its effects on his life were deep and lasting.

The most immediate was that Fred was unable to graduate with his class in June 1946. While the friends with whom he had studied and played for most of his life moved on to their first jobs or, in a few cases, to college, Fred recuperated from his injuries. Then, in the fall of 1946, he went back to Watertown High School to complete the requirements for his degree, which was granted in January 1947. In the long run this may not have mattered much, but at the time it can only have been disrupting and unsettling. Graduating with one's high school class is a milestone in an American life. Fred must have felt cheated of something important, singled out capriciously and isolated from boys and girls about whom he cared a great deal. As in the years ahead he began to become enveloped by a sense of alienation from American society and an inability to live by conventional rules, this cannot have helped.

A second effect of the accident was that it ended his football career. Once his wounds had healed he was able to use his right arm well enough to write, even to play basketball and, in later years, golf, though he carried the arm in a slightly bent position. But football was out of the question. There would be no college football scholarship, no further chance to measure himself against the exacting standards his father had set. In time he would find another arena in which to test himself, but the finality of his rupture from the game he loved must have seemed arbitrary and cruel.

Yet a third consequence of the accident was that when Fred went to Syracuse in the summer of 1951 for his Selective Service physical examination, he was rejected because of his arm. Toward the century's end this may seem a blessing rather than a curse, but in 1951 memories of America's heroic performance in World War II were still fresh. Young American men not merely expected to go into the service—not least because their country still required it of them—but many actively wanted to. Military service, especially in armed combat, was still seen as an honorable and distinctly masculine undertaking, and young men wanted to prove themselves in it. The Korean War had been under way for a year and the United States had suffered some serious reverses, but the sense of purposelessness and human waste that it eventually aroused was only latent then. Fred's buddies were going into the service, his older brother was already in the service, and that was where Fred expected to be. In time, as he began to fall under the spell of 1960s antiwar and anti-American rhetoric, Fred probably came to feel that things had worked out to his advantage. But no one who knew him in 1951 believes that he was happy about his rejection then. It was yet another reason to believe that he was different, a misfit. If his country didn't want him, why should he want his country?

Still, the accident was not without benefits. Charlotte filed a petition on Fred's behalf against Carl J. Hynes, Jean's father, for immediate expenses and long-term damages incurred by Fred in the accident. In December 1947 a New York Supreme Court justice granted Fred "one of the largest uncontested claims in matter of disposition in this county in some time," according to the *Daily Times*. He was awarded total damages of $14,000, of which he received

$9,374.45 after expenses. The court required that $4,987.50 of this be invested in United States Savings Bonds in the names of Charlotte and Fred and placed under supervision of the county clerk, and that the balance of $4,386.95 be deposited in a savings bank in Charlotte's name until Fred turned twenty-one.

Charlotte did not sit tight on Fred's money. She let him have enough of it to buy a secondhand Ford Town & Country sedan with wooden sides, and she permitted much of the rest to underwrite the college education he might otherwise never have received. That was a momentous change in his life. Had he not gone to Southern California, Fred might well have turned into nothing more than the Watertown local character, a ne'er-do-well holding down blue-collar jobs by day and propping up bars by night. Instead he was re-routed on a new path, one that in time directed him into reading and then into making literature.

He was helped along that path, however inadvertently, by a person who probably never would have figured in his life had it not been for the accident on Voodoo Hill. Her name was Jeanne Adams, and she too graduated from Watertown High School in January 1947. Presumably Fred had noticed her earlier—boys couldn't help noticing her, for she was bright and uncommonly pretty—but as members of a small midyear graduating class they saw more of each other than they might otherwise have. They were power-fully attracted to each other. Though Jeanne remembered what passed between them as little more than an intense high school crush, in Fred's mind it was love, "my own first love."

What Fred saw in Jeanne was self-evident to all who knew her. What she saw in him was someone who was funny, who joked a lot, who was good company. Still, they were an unlikely pair. Jeanne was of the Four Hundred. Her father was a high executive at the *Daily Times*; Fred's father was dead, and his mother had not yet made the second marriage that would greatly improve her situation. Beyond that, her parents were old-fashioned and strict, while Fred's father had been notorious for his drinking and Fred was showing signs of heading in the same direction. Even in an age when girls saw little more ahead of them than brief employment followed by marriage and motherhood, Jeanne had far brighter prospects than Fred did.

Still, the romance flourished through graduation and beyond. Fred "worked on the railroad for months, loading great canvas bags of mail onto dolly carts that were taken by freight elevators up to platforms and thrown onto the boxcars of mail trains." It was "dim-witted, backbreaking, brutalizing work," but it was instructive: Fred realized that he wanted more than this, and he decided that he should go to college. Then, as on so many other occasions, Charlotte's sister, Aunt Frances, the same aunt who had sheltered the twins during Earl's final illness, came to the family's assistance. Fred rejoined her and her husband in the fall of 1948 at Golden's Bridge in Westchester County, where he enrolled in a postgraduate course at John Jay High School in Katonah. As well as assuming a heavy academic load, Fred also went out for the basketball team. Not merely did he make it, he became an integral part of what became the first team in the school's history to win its sectional basketball championship, and for his efforts he was named to the conference all-star team. It was his brightest moment of athletic glory, achieved in "what was in many ways the most productive year of my life."

The "overall 86 Regents grade" that Fred received in this course was good enough for Hobart College, which Fred entered in the fall of 1949. The choice was not idle, and it had nothing to do with Earl Exley's brief flirtation with that institution a quarter century earlier. In 1943 Hobart, a men's college, had united with a women's school called William Smith College to form a joint institution known as the Colleges of the Seneca. Though men and women matriculated and lived separately, teachers were appointed to both colleges, and classes were attended by students from both. Jeanne Adams was a student at William Smith, and Fred wanted to join her.

The difficulty was that Jeanne, who had not seen all that much of Fred for some time, had been making a life of her own. More than that, she assumed that things were over between them. Before his sudden arrival at Hobart, Fred had made the dramatic gesture—he was "an intractably inconsolable romantic"—of facing down her father. It was a gentlemanly encounter in which voices were not raised, which must have demanded no small self-control on Fred's part, but nothing that was said could have given Fred any cause for optimism. So Jeanne was surprised when he suddenly showed up at Hobart. She was fond of Fred and not displeased to have him nearby, but the flame had been extinguished. It gratified her that he helped her with an essay that was giving her a hard time, but she was still young and had no interest in anything permanent. Fred, on the other hand, was full of ardor and intent, and pressed her too insistently. Her parents, who may have been the first to find Fred Exley an unsuitable match for their daughter but were hardly the last, insisted that she break it off. Her father was so upset to learn that Fred was in the same town as Jeanne that he had a heart attack, or so Fred claimed at the time. Torn between them and a young man whom she liked but did not love, Jeanne at last told Fred that it, whatever "it" was in his mind, was over. It wasn't easy for her, and she knew it wasn't easy for him, but she scarcely thought it was anything so painful as to change his life.

Fred thought otherwise. He tucked his tail between his legs and went off to Southern California, "because I had been rejected by a girl, my first love, whom I loved beyond the redeeming force of anything save time." He claimed that he once told another "grieving young man" that "it had taken me two years to alleviate the pain, how I had risen with it, gone to bed with it, and lived with it all my waking hours until, accepting its naturalness, it had begun to recede." His separation from Jeanne "was the cause of all my anger, and . . . I was for perhaps a very long time going to have to live with that anger."

Perhaps so, perhaps not. Fred's anger was deep, dark and mysterious. The unrequited love he felt for Jeanne Adams went into his capacious memory, where it joined other wounds and dreams and fears in a place "where I was afraid, afraid of too much beauty and of too much ugliness, afraid of loving and of going unloved, afraid of living and afraid of dying, so afraid of the sun that I could not open my eyes to the morning, and so afraid of the darkness I could not close my eyes to sleep, *afraid*." In this potent mix the loss of Jeanne, the loss of something he had never really had, was a vital part, but there was far more to it than that.

FRED HAD MORE REASON THAN THE END OF HIS ROMANCE with Jeanne to head west. Two years earlier Charlotte, longing for affection and stability, had remarried, to H. Wellington Richardson, known as Wally. He was a decade older than she, a widower with four children, and he was prosperous. The son of a blacksmith, he apprenticed at that trade and pursued it for thirty-two years until, in 1942, he became a partner in the Watertown Spring Service, which manufactured springs for automobiles and trucks. Wartime demands did nothing to hurt the company, nor did the huge consumer market that burst open after the war when rationing stopped.

As a wedding present Wally gave Charlotte a limestone farmhouse at Pamelia Four Corners, a rural spot about ten miles north of Watertown. Known thereafter within the family as "the stone house," always spoken of with reverence and affection, this old building became the center of the Exley-Richardson clan's life and, in time, a place of incalculable importance to Fred—the most important building in his life, it is no exaggeration to say. Also in time, Fred came to understand Wally's "dignity, kindness, and constancy," and to pay powerfully moving tribute to him in *A Fan's Notes,* but this understanding was many years in the making. In the late 1940s Fred resented the stranger in his mother's bed, missed the father with whom he had never wholly reconciled, and was beginning a long, slow descent into what would almost certainly now be identified as depression. All he wanted was to get away.

That the place to which he fled was the University of Southern California seems, at first glance, inexplicable. Inasmuch as Fred's reputation rests on literary achievement, one would expect him to have chosen a university distinguished in that regard; but in the fall of 1950 literature surely was the last thing on Fred's mind. Like countless other Watertown residents before and since, he wanted to flee cold and isolation for warmth and urbanity. The prospect of sitting in the Rose Bowl and watching one of the country's perpetual football powers might have appealed to him, though he claimed that he never saw Frank Gifford play football during his three years there. Whether he tried other California schools is not recorded—Stanford and Berkeley leap immediately to mind as places that would have attracted him—but Southern Cal is where he went. He was happy there, if not necessarily happy in the terms most people define the word: contented, at ease, at peace.

This is not the impression he was eager to give. Southern Cal was "a large, undistinguished university in Los Angeles," he said, and he liked to pound away at its reputation "as the place where rich kids from Beverly Hills came if they were too dumb to get into Stanford." He claimed that in his senior year "I dated a beautiful girl whose mother, when I finally came to meet her, actually said to me, 'We're Standard Oil of California,' to which, had not the girl smiled and winked at me, I almost responded, 'I'm Niagara Mohawk of Upstate New York.' " He portrayed himself as a habitué of the 901 Club on Jefferson Boulevard, "the hangout for drunken WWII veterans (they had a 24-hour-a-day poker game that lasted all my years there), manque poets, aspiring novelists, petulant young instructors, etc."

Fred went to California with the intention, however ludicrous it may sound, of studying dentistry, but he soon found his way to the English Department, "with a view to reading The Books, The Novels and The Poems, those pat reassurances that other men had experienced rejection and pain and loss." Later he remembered himself as "cutting across the neat-cropped grass of the campus, burdened down by the weight of the books in which I sought the consolation of other men's grief, and burdened further by the large weight of my own bitterness." It is a mistake to take this literally. Whatever Fred may have sought in the reading he began to attack with such immense appetite, he found far more than he had bargained for.

What he found was his vocation. By his own confession this was for a long time more sentimental dream than reality, but the desire to write was provoked in him by the reading he did, in class and on his own, at Southern California. Something that stuck with him over the years was the admonition by a visiting professor of literature that "books do not get written on the Montparnasse," that it is one thing to talk about writing and quite another to do it. For a long time Fred was a captive of the illusion that "the vibrant, incessant hum" of the literati was evidence of "plays, paintings, and novels just short of being realized," but eventually he realized that there was no substitute for the work itself, and he started to do it. The seed for that decision had been planted at Southern Cal.

The importance that this institution played in Fred's life is suggested by the resentment he felt over its indifference to his literary success. In 1978 he wrote to a professor whose classes in creative writing and the American novel Fred had attended. "I was a lackadaisical, slovenly student but think I managed to get a B in both courses," he said. There were a couple of other professors whose influence he acknowledged: "Talking with college graduates my age, I find that remembering three professors is rather better than average. Most of them can only remember one or two who had any significant impact on their lives."

Having thus disposed of the obligation to flatter, Fred then turned to the real business of his letter. He was the author of two volumes of a trilogy, the first the winner of two awards, the second "considered for but did *not* win a Pulitzer Prize." He had "read at any number of colleges and have always felt rather slighted that I was never asked back to my alma mater." Moreover: "Two years ago, in the Lion's Head in Greenwich Village, a watering hole where young people come to gawk at their drunken, egomaniacal idols, I was approached by a young lady, a recent USC alumna, who told me she knew of at least two young instructors who were teaching me out there. This made me feel even more slighted!" Then, rising to the full height of his Fredness, he made the inevitable pitch:

> In any event, in April I'm going out to Evanston, thence to Iowa City to read from my work in progress and would like

to continue on to USC if it can be worked out. As my plane fare from Syracuse to Chicago is already taken care of, I'd need a round trip from Chicago to LA, some suitable remuneration and two days in the faculty club or a motel. I ask for two days because I haven't been back there since my graduation in 1953 and would like to spend a day walking around the campus. I hope you are well and thank you both for your teaching and for your consideration.

Nothing came of this shameless solicitation—not that shame was a sentiment with which Fred, in his business dealings, ever was acquainted—but that is a pity. Fred's manner may have been obsequiously peremptory, but the desire for recognition from his old school was genuine. He had come there a child of the Depression, the lineman's son, and had withstood indifference and snobbery in the process of discovering important things about himself. He had made no dent on the campus but the campus had made one on him, and now that he had achieved a measure of fame elsewhere it was time that he be recognized.

This was not an unreasonable request. Southern California is a considerably more reputable academic institution than its fame as a football factory would suggest, and its library's collection of American literature is said to be excellent, but it is not known as a spawning place for writers. Letting Fred Exley read on campus would have made him happy—deliriously so, in all likelihood—at small expense, and the connection between the man and the institution would have been a flower in the lapel of the latter. But universities are as insensate as the buildings that house them, and arrogant into the bargain; Fred's plea was made into unheeding ears.

Still, Southern Cal had already given him much more than he could have expected when he went there. He had his reflexive complaints about the fraternities and the rich kids, but the hours in class and the reading required for them had opened his eyes to worlds he never knew. He became then and remained for the rest of his life a reader, at least as much as he was a writer. He read all day and all night, in the process gradually becoming one of those people for whom the line between the world of books and the world of reality is indistinguishable. Reviewing *Pages from a Cold Island,* Alfred Kazin wrote in *The New York Times Book Review* that Fred "cares for nothing but storytelling, has evidently read nothing but novels, and wouldn't recognize the unfabled, unvarnished, non-smart truth if it hit him." This was not kindly meant and is not wholly true, but in essence it is accurate; once his first book had been written, Fred lived more for the words he could make out of his life than for life itself. The world of books became a retreat into which Fred fled, a place where he achieved a presence and an authority that the real world denied him. Those may have been the only terms on which he could live out his days. Whatever the case, the University of Southern California made him—or let him make himself—what he was.

His B.A. in English was awarded in the spring of 1953. His family assumed that he would return to Watertown and begin to lead a normal life. Perhaps he would teach English at one of the local schools. But the Exleys did not know that the unexpected child was about to take an unexpected turn. Those hours at the 901 Club and other bohemian hangouts had given Fred a taste for the unconventional life that precisely suited the unconventional side of himself. The boy who had been lost in the crowd at Watertown High School and at Southern California was now a young man, albeit an immature one, and he was turning into someone quite unlike anyone Watertown had ever before seen.

He didn't hang around Watertown for long. Instead he made the hegira that young Americans of intelligence, curiosity and ambition had been making for generations. He went to New York City. In *A Fan's Notes* he claims that he suffered months of rejection and frustration that ended only when "I combed my hair, had my suit cleaned, walked into the personnel department of the New York Central Railroad, and told the man I would take anything he had to offer." This is only partly true. There may have been a long period of failure, but the job at the railroad quite certainly did not come about in the fashion thus described. Aunt Frances's husband, Ernest Knapp, was a figure of consequence at the New York Central, head of its Harlem Division. He had the power to hire and to influence others in other departments to do so as well, which surely is what happened in Fred's case. He was taken on as a clerk-trainee in the passenger department and soon promoted to the public relations department. He "bought a couple tweed suits, a few delicately patterned bow ties, and a pair of sincere black Oxfords"; inasmuch as Fred was rarely thereafter seen in suit and tie, the effort must be made to visualize him as he was then, however briefly, a young man in a suit, Brooks Brothers if not gray flannel, attempting to conform to middle-class expectations of the mid-1950s.

By the end of 1954 Fred had been transferred to the Central's Chicago office, but this assignment lasted only a couple of weeks before his job was eliminated. At loose ends in a city he scarcely knew, Fred felt "something very like despair," but that didn't last long, either. Before he could clear out his office Ted Zirbes, public relations director for the Rock Island Railroad, dropped by to introduce himself. When Fred admitted that he no longer had a job at the Central, Zirbes said, "Don't worry about it. C'mon down and work for me." That is what Fred did. As the *Watertown Daily Times* reported in February 1955, "Fred E. Exley is the new managing editor of the Rock Island's employee magazine, 'The Rocket.' . . . In addition to his duties as managing editor, Mr. Exley will serve as public relations representative."

So Fred found living quarters on the near North Side and began work at the last job apart from schoolteaching he ever held for more than a few months. His first published writing appeared in *The Rocket,* which gave great pleasure to his family and probably encouraged Charlotte in her vain hope of a "normal" future for him. That was never in the cards. Fred may have started at the Rock Island in a burst of enthusiasm, but other matters interested him far more. He was living in a city charged with energy and possibility, at a time when that city and the nation itself were changing in ways few then understood.

The 1950s are commonly portrayed as a period of conformity, boosterism and political repression. Plenty of that was in the air, but there was also a nascent resistance against it, and in few places was it stronger than in Chicago. By 1955 the Korean War was over, in an inconclusive peace that left some Americans doubting, for the first time since World War II, the wisdom of sending American troops to foreign conflicts that did not seem to involve the country's immediate interests. The *Brown* v. *Board of Education* ruling by the

Supreme Court had put the law on the side of equal rights, but the reaction to it had persuaded some people that it would take far more than court decisions to eradicate prejudice and its effects. Senator Joseph McCarthy's heyday was over, but the effects of his anti-Communist witch-hunt were still widely felt among the intelligentsia, whose members wondered whether independent thought and speech were possible in a climate of fear and anger.

Fred Exley was not really a political creature, though he had a storehouse of political opinions, but he was deeply touched by the wave of skepticism that swept through the thinking classes during the time he was in Chicago. Among the smart young people with whom he drank and talked at North Side saloons and clubs—Larry's, Gus's, Mister Kelly's—sarcasm and insouciance were all the rage. Like Lenny Bruce, to whose recordings they listened time after time, Fred and his friends considered themselves "too hip for the room," and competed with one another to see who could get off the most telling comments on public figures, middle-class vulgarity and all the usual targets. These people weren't intellectuals; they worked in public relations jobs like Fred's, or at advertising agencies, or in stockbrokerages. But they had been to college, they were hip and self-aware, they kept up with the new music and the new books.

As to the latter, there was plenty to talk about. Faulkner and Hemingway were still around, but the former remained a mystery to most readers, and the latter, in the opinion of these North Side twentysomething critics, was an "asshole"; they made wisecracks about his mannered language—"Did the earth move for you last night?"—and dismissed his macho posturing, though for one of them it was to prove an irresistible exemplar in years to come. The authors who interested them were the Young Turks or, in the words of one of those authors, "the young lions." That was Irwin Shaw. Along with Norman Mailer and James Jones, he had war stories to tell that struck young readers as far more realistic and true than Hemingway's labored miniatures. A first novel called *Lie Down in Darkness* by a young Virginian, William Styron, jolted them with its vivid account of drunkenness and self-destruction among his home state's gentry. Close to home, a hugely ambitious picaresque novel by Saul Bellow, *The Adventures of Augie March,* made Chicago a subject to be reckoned with.

"I am an American, Chicago born—Chicago, that somber city—and go at things as I have taught myself, free-style...first to knock, first admitted...." Fred read Bellow's famous opening words in 1953 or 1954, and they echoed in his mind ever after. He read *Augie March* "till it came unbound and the pages started dropping out." To his pals in North Side saloons he proclaimed, over and over, that "*Augie March* is the greatest fuckin' book." Its panoramic view of the American experience appealed to Fred's romantic side, and its sharp critique of certain aspects of bourgeois life struck agreeable notes on his sardonic side. The book became his constant companion; it was, along with Vladimir Nabokov's *Lolita,* the greatest influence on his own work.

In the company of all these hip young people, Fred was at home. It was the 901 Club moved to the Middle West, with suits and ties replacing jeans and khakis. The Chicagoans got together at saloons and at cocktail parties, where they munched on canapés and drank in copious amounts. None drank more than Fred Exley.

✧

In Fred's legend, nothing yields pride of place to his drinking. There are people who knew him for years and never, to their knowledge, saw him sober. He drank when he got up, he drank all day long, he drank lying in bed. He liked food, especially Italian dishes, but when it came to a choice between the two there was never any doubt, and he didn't always remember whether any choice had been made. Once in his later years an acquaintance from out of town went with his wife and a few friends to a restaurant on Wellesley Island in the St. Lawrence, where Fred was in residence. The visitor saw Fred at the bar.

"Fred, how you doin'?"

"Good, Bill."

"What's goin' on?"

"Not much."

"Well, we're going to have dinner. Why don't you join us?"

"Why should I do that?"

"We'd enjoy your company."

Fred stayed at the bar. A while later the visitor again urged Fred to join his party. "Would it be all right?" Fred asked. "Of course." So Fred picked up his drink and shuffled over to the table. He sat down and exchanged small talk with the man and his guests. Finally the waitress appeared and began to take orders. Fred wasn't interested. He sat sipping his drink and taking in the scene. But the visitor persisted.

"Fred, why don't you have something?"

"Well, all right," Fred said. "Maybe I'll order a salad just in case I haven't eaten."

His drinking started in high school. South of town was a place across the street from the New Parrot where sixteen-year-olds had no trouble getting ten-cent draft beer. This got Fred into the beer habit and the bar habit, both of which stayed with him for life. He loved the camaraderie of the bar, and from the outset he knew how to run a tab; if there are people who never saw him sober, there are also people who never saw him pay cash for a drink. Like a place to sleep and a ticket to ride, booze was one of Fred's entitlements.

He drank beer throughout his life, but most of the time his drink of choice was vodka, often taken with grapefruit juice. Vodka became a popular drink in this country for the first time in the 1950s, in large measure due to a clever Smirnoff's advertising campaign. It became especially popular among people who didn't like the taste of alcohol but either wanted the effects of it or felt that social circumstances required them to drink. Fred was almost certainly one of the former. In the many passages he wrote about drinking, and in the many stories that have been told about his drinking, the missing element is always pleasure. Fred liked the conviviality that drinking produced and he liked the effects it had on him, but he didn't like drink itself. He drank cheap vodka and mediocre beer. During the period in the 1980s when he lived in an apartment over Clark Reidel's garage on Wellesley Island, Fred once exhausted his host's supply of expensive beer and went to a liquor store to replace it; there were actually times when Fred paid for his drinks and settled the tabs he ran at the bars he patronized. Fred came back from his errand with two cases of Heineken's and fire in his eyes.

"What's wrong, Fred?"

"That stuff's twenty-seven dollars a case! Get Genny Light from now on!"

In his mind Fred could not "divorce the term *alcoholism* from *sadness*." Although there were many reasons why he drank, the most important arose from his need to tone down internal antennae that were too sensitive. Those who knew him best testify to the remarkable and often painful depth of his perceptions as well as to the terrible degree to which memory haunted him. No one knew this better than Fred himself:

> After a month's sobriety my faculties became unbearably acute and I found myself unhealthily clairvoyant, having insights into places I'd as soon not journey to. Unlike some men, I have never drunk for boldness or charm or wit; I had used alcohol for precisely what it was, a depressant to check the mental exhilaration produced by extended sobriety.

Not merely did Fred see too much, he remembered too much. He was beset by "debilitating dreams, ancient insults, past hurts inflicted . . . all the things that ravage a soul and age the body, that turn the eyes inward and settle a melancholy on the countenance." One night at the Lion's Head, drinking at a table with a half-dozen people, Fred suddenly said, "I remember about ten years ago, we were sitting at this table talking about movies." He then recapitulated in exact detail a conversation that had taken place a decade before. As the memories flowed forth his companions muttered, "God, that's right, I said that."

It is astonishing not merely that he remembered all those lost and forgotten words but that he had been drunk when he heard them. Everything he saw and heard entered his memory and stayed there, to torment him beyond his capacity to bear it. One way he faced up to these demons was to write about them, directly or at an angle. The other way was to drink them into oblivion, however temporary that might prove to be.

He did not drink when he wrote. "I've never written a single line on the booze," he said, "or even with a hangover. I mean, I've taken a lot of notes, but when it comes down to the nitty-gritty, it's either shit or get off the pot." If he was drinking and saw or heard something he might want to use in his writing, he scrawled a note to himself on any scrap of paper that happened to be handy; when he got back to whatever passed for home at the time, he tossed the scrap into a box filled with others. But if he was on the sauce, he made no effort to turn observation into literature. Instead he mustered up all his determination and went on the wagon.

When he was young this was comparatively easy, but the older he got the harder it became. Clark and Bobbi Reidel, with whom Fred lived in the late 1980s, were occasional witnesses to, and participants in, the drying-out process. It began with Fred's declaration, "I'm quitting on Monday," at which point he turned off the vodka and started "tapering off," as he called it, on beer. In the worst of times he went through hallucinations and had to be nursed through them; he sweated and shivered and drank gallons of ice water and orange juice. Once the drying-out process was complete, he was a new man. His speech didn't change much; he always droned in a monotone and always slurred his words. But he suddenly developed a keen interest in his health and went on long walks, as much as ten miles a day. On Wellesley Island he took up golf; the manager of the Thousand

Islands Golf Club let him play for free if he was sober, which was a great deal for Fred because when he was drunk he didn't want to play anyway.

Golf or walking was for the morning. He went home at midday, slept until early evening, puttered around for a while, then went back to sleep. At midnight or thereabouts he began writing, and stayed at his desk, drinking coffee and writing. One of these dry spells lasted for eight or nine months, then ended suddenly when a minor disruption in his life set off all the old alarms; the one certainty about Fred was that sooner or later he'd be back on the bottle.

In *A Fan's Notes* Fred mentions in passing his "idiotic pretense that I was not a drunk," but he knew that he was one and made no effort to hide or disguise it. In San Francisco in 1976 he was invited to lunch at the penthouse of a wealthy and prominent woman named Pat Montandon. Paul Hemphill was then a columnist for the *San Francisco Examiner,* for which he wrote about the occasion a couple of days later:

> Pat Montandon is this elegant woman who throws a "round-table luncheon" as often as she can. She invites eight or ten "interesting" people and they drink and eat and sit around discussing "important" things. The luncheons become Radical Chic after a while. At any rate, Wednesday there was authoress Jessica Mitford and an effeminate clergyman and a founder of a women's liberation organization and other showy people. Pat Montandon was, as is the custom, asking everyone to tell about themselves. Exley, this crazy novelist, was becoming crazier as his turn approached. When the time came for him to explain himself he abruptly stood up and blurted, "My name is Fred Ex. I am an alcoholic," and sat down.

Fred's drinking in Chicago was heavy, but no one paid much attention to it because he traveled in hard-drinking circles. He did cause talk one evening at Larry's when he got into an argument with a nurse who was his bedmate of the moment. She was "a lousy fucking cunt," he shouted, and then tried to barge out the door. It wouldn't move, so he kicked furiously at it. The glass panel broke, cutting his toe severely. Blood was all over the place. Fred was rushed to a hospital and stitched back together.

The women in Fred's life and the treatment they received from him will be discussed shortly. Here two points are pertinent. The first is that in his crowd the flashy young men had eyes for flashy young women. Nurses, showgirls and stewardesses were abundant, as well as others advertising their charms for one of the flashiest of these young men, Hugh Hefner, whose new magazine, *Playboy,* was beginning to find readers, or lookers, and to exercise an incalculable influence on American sexual mores. These were the women—easy come, easy go—with whom Fred hung out. This leads to the second point, which is that there is no evidence that Fred had a serious girlfriend during his Chicago period. Thus Bunny Sue Allorgee, the pivotal female figure in *A Fan's Notes,* gives every sign of being a creation of Fred's imagination. Like Robin Glenn in *Last Notes from Home,* she appears to have been drawn from, and fantasized upon, several women whom Fred had known.

Women in any event were always less important to Fred than booze and bars. He was happiest when holding forth from his barstool; he regaled listeners not with anecdotes— he was not really a raconteur—but with ad-lib monologues: wry, sarcastic, shapeless commentaries on people he had known in Watertown, people in the Chicago crowd, people in the news. His humor could be merciless to those at whom it was directed, but they were rarely in the room when he took aim. He was a bluffer rather than a fighter, and preferred to give offense *in absentia.*

Among Fred's most avid listeners was Jerome Raskin, a young Chicagoan working in an advertising agency. He and Fred both were in their mid-twenties, both were working in jobs that did not interest them, both were given to talk about writers and books, to what Raskin called "the pretentious talk of twenty-four-year-old guys." One way they expressed their discontent was to walk out on their jobs at midday and meet at a nearby movie house to attend the matinee. They especially liked the films of James Dean and Marlon Brando, the folk heroes of 1950s rebellion, but whatever was playing was fine with them, whether it was a John Wayne Western or a Claude Rains suspense film.

By 1956 Fred's indifference to normal working hours and his steady drunkenness cost him his job. He quit his apartment and moved in with Jerry Raskin, whom he regularly hit for "loans" that were never repaid; these weren't for large amounts, just enough to keep Fred in whatever beer he couldn't get someone else to pay for. Soon Raskin decided that he wanted to revisit Arizona, where he had gone to preparatory school, and look into possible real estate investments. Fred, who was unencumbered by chattels or anything else, was happy to tag along. "No one ever loved a city the way I loved that place," but Chicago had nothing more to offer Fred. So in the winter of 1956–57 he climbed into Jerry's Aston Martin and headed west.

They arrived in Phoenix, found an apartment and stayed there for three months. Jerry went out to explore opportunities—he found them, and settled down for good—but Fred planted himself in the apartment and stayed planted. He turned on the television set and left it on. "I almost never watch television," he said, "but I never turn it off either"; a humming television in the background was to become a constant in his existence, "in the way one puts a ticking clock in a six-week-old puppy's pillowed box to assure him that Mom is always there." He lounged around in his underwear, flipping cigarette ashes with his thumb, every once in a while calling for a few more dollars to tide him over. Finally even Raskin—for whom "Fred could do no wrong"—had as much as he could stand. Like everyone upon whose hospitality Fred imposed, Jerry kicked him out. He drove him to Los Angeles, and dropped him at a friend's house. For a while Jerry hung around with Fred in Los Angeles. They went to clubs where Shorty Rogers, Gerry Mulligan and others were adding the "cool" West Coast sound to the jazz repertoire—the clubs were less appealing to Fred for the jazz than for the booze—and on sightseeing tours of Schwab's drugstore, the Garden of Allah and other Hollywood attractions, but soon Jerry went back to the real world. Fred stayed where he was, on a slow journey back to Watertown and Mom.

He worked briefly as "a publicist for the missile systems division of a large aircraft corporation," Lockheed, but quit that after a while and hit the road again. He was in Colorado briefly, then in New York, where he ran into his brother, who did not like what he saw. Bill thought Fred was drinking too much and was concerned that he might be mentally unbalanced; he was especially worried that Fred might bring unnecessary anguish and grief to their mother. So Bill urged him to come to Baltimore, where he was then stationed, "and stay with us for a while." Judy, Bill's wife, had not met Fred before but had heard enough about him to assume that he wasn't running on all cylinders and to adopt the standard family line: That's Freddie.

In Baltimore, Fred did what in those days he did everywhere: he loafed around all day, called for service when it was required, drank up everything in the house. When there seemed to be no more liquor or beer around, Bill told Judy, "Don't buy anything else," but Fred managed to track down a bottle of crème de menthe, which he meted out in his morning coffee. Finally Bill got through to him, and helped him find a job as bartender at the Corral Inn in Dundalk, the working-class neighborhood where they lived. It wasn't the best imaginable employment for an alcoholic; Fred soon got himself fired for drinking on the job, as he subsequently did at a second bar that inexplicably agreed to take him on.

Fred was in Baltimore for the usual stretch, about three months. At last Bill had had all he could take. He packed Fred's suitcase and put it, and Fred, out on the sidewalk. Never one to complain about such minor inconveniences, Fred pointed south, to "that sunny cesspool Miami, where I worked for two hours as a dishwasher but was too weak from not eating to get the big pans clean, and where I was confronted by [a] tart-tongued judge and given the choice of coming up with some money or going to the county farm." Instead Fred appealed to Charlotte, who—"correctly surmising that I'd never board the airplane if she sent cash"—bought him a plane ticket back to Watertown.

He arrived at the stone house in the fall of 1957. He collapsed on his mother's davenport, "staring at the ceiling and dreaming my dreams," and stayed there until the spring of the next year.

IT IS HERE, AS WE APPROACH THE CENTER OF THE STORY OF Fred's life, that we must pause to ask its central question: What drove him to his mother's davenport? What was it— the "wound," the "rage"—that rendered him helpless in the conventional world, that isolated him in a universe of his own and then drove him to attempt to heal that wound by writing one of the masterly books of his time?

The question has no conclusive answer. The chances are that Fred himself could not have answered it, though in *A Fan's Notes* he shrugs it off by calling himself "one mad dreamer out of the cold, cow country up yonder," suggesting that his problem was lunacy rather than maladjustment or chronic unhappiness. From time to time, to be sure, he drops hints. In *A Fan's Notes* he describes telling a psychiatrist about "something from my past that I had told to no one before him, nor will ever tell again," and says no more. In *Last Notes from Home* he describes in painful detail—we have no way of knowing whether the story is true or invented—his betrayal of a girl who, when both were young, had given her virginal self to him, and writes: "What happened that night, as well as the repercussions therefrom, I would shut from my mind for years. I could not have functioned in the world otherwise." Inasmuch as the second passage was written at least two decades after the first, the possibility that Fred had decided to speak the unspeakable cannot be dismissed; this incident may have been what had permanently altered him.

But taking Fred at his word is the easy way out. To accuse an innocent, vulnerable, trusting girl of being a whore is terrible, but in and of itself it is hardly enough. Fred's wound was too deep and too wide to permit easy identification. It may have had a single cause, but it far more likely had many explanations, all pointed in the same direction.

The most revealing and important words Fred wrote are where one would expect to find them, in *A Fan's Notes.* They occur when Fred, at Southern California, bumps into Frank Gifford at a campus hamburger joint:

> He was dressed in blue denims and a terry-cloth sweater, and though I saw no evidence of *USC* stamped anyplace, still I had an overwhelming desire to insult him in some way. How this would be accomplished with any subtlety I had no idea; I certainly didn't want to fight with him. I did, however, want to shout, "Listen, you son of a bitch, life isn't all a goddam football game! You won't always get the girl! Life is rejection and pain and loss." . . .

Fred immediately softened those words by calling them "all those things I cherishingly cuddled in my self-pitying bosom," but this is one case in which his attempt at confession must be seen as a diversionary technique rather than an exploration of the truth. "Rejection and pain and loss" are the keys to any understanding of Fred Exley, for it was the agony caused by these that was at the very heart of him.

Over and over again Fred was rejected, or—and in his case there is no significant difference—believed himself to have been rejected. He was humiliated, at the defenseless age of thirteen, by his father. He was spurned by Jeanne Adams at the insistence of her parents. He lost the ability to play football. He was turned down by the armed forces. His sexual life was certainly troubled and probably unsatisfactory. Above all, he was an irreconcilable misfit in the place he loved more than any other.

Because we have only Fred's side of the story, we can do no more than guess at the true nature of the relationship between him and his father. Both of Fred's sisters recall Earl Exley as affectionate and caring but distracted, his real life being outside the family rather than within it. To an overly sensitive soul such as Fred, a boy desperate for his father's love and approval, blameless actions on Earl's part may have taken on an import that bore little relationship to Earl's actual intent. But what matters is what Fred felt, not what Earl said or did, and it is clear not merely that he felt neglected but that his failure to reach an understanding with Earl before his death left within him the doubt, which must have been excruciating, that an understanding could ever have been reached. There can be little question that Fred turned the story of himself and Earl into a literary device, or that he elaborated upon it for dramatic purposes, but by the same token there can be little question that what he wrote is essentially the truth, that the ache for his father never left him.

The ache for Jeanne Adams may never have left him either. Inasmuch as there seems never to have been a woman in Fred's life who provided an exact model for Bunny Sue Allorgee, it does not seem unreasonable to hazard that his longing for Jeanne provided the raw material from which Bunny Sue emerged. In no way is this to suggest that there are similarities between Bunny Sue and Jeanne as individuals or between Fred's fictional relationship with Bunny Sue and his actual one with Jeanne. But Jeanne Adams, as a woman and as a member of Watertown's upper crust, embodied things for which Fred yearned—beauty, warmth, love, respect, poise—and which he was denied when she ended their romance. Whether consciously or not, by losing his potency with Bunny Sue and thus rejecting her in the most intimate way, Fred turned the tables: *he* became, however perversely, the figure of power whose "sexual failure in the end redeemed me, saved me from an almost certain castration" by a woman who would domesticate and thus Americanize him. Bunny Sue assumes two vital functions: she is the America that Fred claimed to despise, and she is his revenge on the girl—as well as the girl's parents—who would not have him, who said, or so he interpreted it, that the lineman's son was not good enough for her.

The two wounds caused by Fred's automobile accident— his removal from the football field and his rejection by the army—are the least injurious. If he thought he had any future as an athlete, he was a fool, and in matters such as that he was not foolish. The Watertown High School football season of 1945 would have been his last whether or not the accident had occurred, unless he could have found a college that would let him play. It may have hurt him that football, which gave him pleasure, would thenceforth be off-limits, but in the best of circumstances his football future was dim, so the hurt must have been slight.

The same goes for the army. If on the one hand Fred hated yet another rejection, as well as being denied entry to a place where many of his best friends were going, on the other hand it seems a remote possibility that Fred Exley, who by 1951 had developed a healthy disregard for authority and regimentation in any form, really looked forward with enthusiasm to the prospect of two compulsory years at an institution that subjected those herded within it to daily indignities designed to suppress their individuality.

So there we have four wounds, two large, two small. Taken together they add up to a lot of rejection and pain and loss, some lasting for a long time. If Fred really believed that he had been rejected *by* his father and then rejected by Jeanne and her parents *because* he was his father's son, that could be a potent mix. But potent enough to drive him into a state of perpetual quarantine, to leave him embittered beyond hope of reconciliation and wounded beyond prospect of cure? Isn't that a bit much to ascribe to hurtful rebuffs such as many people suffer and from which most in time recover? We have to look deeper than that: to sources within the man himself, aspects of him that cannot be changed because they are bred in the bone.

This brings us to a question that was posed by a man who knew Fred well, who was exasperated by him as everyone else was but who liked him and admired his writing. For many years, he said, he had mused about Fred's "wound," and had finally found himself wondering whether it had anything to do with repressed or uncertain sexual identity. Was Fred Exley as unhappy as he was, this man asked, because he denied or doubted his essential nature?

Opinions on this were solicited from many of Fred's other friends, producing reactions that ranged from shocked or amused denial to tentative, uncertain agreement. No one thought that Fred ever had a homosexual encounter— though how could anyone have known?—and many found it impossible to believe that he ever entertained homosexual longings or inclinations. But there was wide agreement that his sexual life, such as anyone knows of it, was peculiar, that his attitudes toward and treatment of women were often those of a man who did not like women, and that his Hemingwayesque sexual persona contained elements suggesting less confidence in himself than his blustery strutting was meant to convey.

This is shaky ground, but it deserves to be explored within the narrow limits of what we know about Fred as a sexual creature. Though at times he sought to portray himself as sensitive about sex and the feelings of the women with whom he had it, there is considerable evidence to the contrary. Women with whom he slept described him as a perfunctory partner whose only real interest was his own gratification, the speedier the better; men commented that he saw women as little more than "vessels" for the jism he discharged. In *Pages from a Cold Island* he repeatedly refers to his penis as "the frightful hog" and attempts to mythologize its potency and prowess, yet there is remarkably little, in that book or anything else he wrote for public or private consumption, about putting this instrument to customary heterosexual use. Instead there are repeated references to oral sex, performed by Fred or on Fred, that imply a fixation upon this form of gratification going far beyond the customary boundaries of sexual activity.

A selection of Fred's musings and braggadocio on this subject is necessary to illustrate the point, however tedious and distasteful it may be. We must bear in mind that an essential ingredient of Fred's humor was outrageousness, and that some of what he wrote may therefore have been with tongue in cheek. Still, the evidence is overwhelming.

In *A Fan's Notes* references to oral sex are infrequent, though much of the long "Mr. Blue" section revolves around it: "He had some deranged notion of the typical housewife slinking about all day in a reeky housecoat, chain-smoking, scratching her 'hairy ass,' and undesistingly yearning for oral stimulation of her labia. 'That's all they think about!' Mr. Blue said. 'It's a *thing* with them!' " Inasmuch as Mr. Blue is introduced for satirical and metaphorical purposes—Fred had the idea that he was America in miniature—it stands to reason that his cunnilingual obsession is similarly intended.

In *Pages from a Cold Island,* though, Fred himself becomes the champion "lapper," to borrow Mr. Blue's felicitous coinage. Fred writes about offering to service orally "a Bennington coed with whom I'd exchanged three or four letters," to "induce from her a half-dozen orgasms before even showing her . . . 'the frightful hog,' " and to "emit on her teeth, her eyeballs, her breasts, her ass and whatever else she owned she was particularly proud of." Watching television, he shouts at an actress in a dramatic series: "Atta girl! Atta way! Blow him! Ream him! Give him a head job that'll make that paradise he's going to look pale by comparison!" In Nassau he lies on a beach with a wayward wife who "took down my bathing suit and with her mouth engaged me. She did this all day long, and did the same for the next three days. She'd absorb the load, lay [*sic*] back, leaving her hand on my exposed genitalia, then after a time begin all over again." Preparing for an interview with the feminist Gloria Steinem, he is asked by her representative what his purpose is and fantasizes about answering: "Oh, I don't know, my dear. I haven't as yet decided what I want with Ms. Steinem. It may be as simple as that I'll want to fuck her face for her."

If one of the cumulative effects of these brief extracts is to provide embarrassing proof of just how vulgar a book *Pages from a Cold Island* really is, another obviously is to emphasize that oral sex was not merely a proclivity with Fred but an obsession. The same point is made in *Last Notes from Home*. He imagines the pilots of commercial airliners lying in far-away motel rooms "erupting into the hot moist mouths of lovely young attendants, those glorified and somehow touching hash slingers of the heavens." To Fred himself, the unimaginably fetching Robin Glenn, a flight attendant, says, "I want to suck your cock." In what he calls "the most explosively erotic scene to which I've ever been a party," a woman named Alissa goes down on him: ". . . your russet hair came down spreading like a silken web over my lap, I gently stroked the back of your head, and then, at last and finally, I came." Then there is Cass McIntyre, the girl whom he betrays, who before offering herself to him moves "to her knees before me" in the dark of a movie theater and gives him his first experience of fellatio, leaving him unable to "accurately describe my unbridled terror, my immeasurable anguish, my boundless pleasure" at what, he seems to have recognized from the first, was his true sexual pleasure.

A woman who knew Fred well in an entirely platonic way and who loved him dearly suggested that he may not have enjoyed physical contact, with women or anyone else. It is true that he was in unexpected ways a persnickety man—his living quarters were always fussily neat and his clothes, however sloppy, were almost always clean and pressed—who in some respects had an antiseptic approach to life and, perhaps, to love. Yet if oral sex does not involve genital penetration, it isn't exactly antiseptic, either. It is difficult not to conclude that there was something about the ordinary heterosexual act that Fred found unpleasant, or worse, and that oral sex was a way of gratifying himself while at the same time avoiding it.

This suspicion is strengthened by an impressive body of evidence leading to an intimately related point: that Fred tolerated women at best and loathed them at worst. By way of transition, consider this passage from a letter Fred wrote, and may or may not have sent, to a woman who aspired to be a writer. He urged her to look up a friend of his at the Lion's Head saloon in Greenwich Village: ". . . if he assures me you look any good I'll invite you down . . . and give you the privilege of sucking my cock, providing you don't bring any manuscript for me to read. If he doesn't hear from you, I'll assume that you're like every other cunt I know with literary pretensions, uglier than shit."

That nasty document, bringing together on one sheet of paper Fred's fetish for oral sex and his animus toward women, takes us to his dark side. It is true that Fred may often have resorted to cunnilingus because of impotence induced by alcohol, but it is also true that Fred was more than just what many of his friends called him, a "man's man." He was also a man with a troubled and ambivalent attitude toward the opposite sex, a man whose mind was filled with images of violence against women that occasionally became reality, a man who seemed genuinely comfortable only with women who presented no sexual opportunity, challenge or threat.

Fred's dealings with women were almost never easy. To be sure, he aroused a powerful maternal instinct, to which many women attested and of which other men took note; the perpetual little boy, or great big baby, he made many women want to protect him. He was also shy with women, as a boy and as an adult, to which some women responded with a similar protectiveness. He was not confident about asking women on dates or trying to pick them up, and didn't mind letting others run interference for him.

If there were these hints of diffidence and timidity, there were even stronger ones of indifference and hostility. He was rarely seen at the Lion's Head with a woman, much less one who appeared to be a lover, and the same was true of the bars he frequented late in his life at Alexandria Bay. Considering that he hung around with a self-consciously macho crowd, it is remarkable how few men can recall his engaging in standard-issue locker-room conversations about women. There is a prevailing sense among them that the sex scenes in his books, the last two in particular, are almost entirely imaginary; in actuality he went off to the Lion's Head or someplace else, got drunk, and came back alone to wherever he was staying.

If anything, for a man who wrote so graphically about what he represented as his sex life, his interest in women bordered on nonexistent. Once David Markson invited Fred and another habitué of the Lion's Head to dinner at his flat in Greenwich Village. Markson's wife, Elaine, fixed the meal in the kitchen while the men chatted in the living room. At meal's end Fred's first words were: "Well! Wanna go to the Head?" So far as he was concerned the woman had been on hand solely to meet his needs, and this entailed no obligation to sit around after dinner engaging her in polite conversation. It was time to get back to his real world, of booze and guys.

The line between indifference and overt hostility was thin. Fred hit both of his wives. As a couple of his friends pointed out, these days we are alert to aspects of marriage that alarmed relatively few people a generation ago. Fred wasn't the only one of his crowd who hit his wife, so what he did should be viewed in context, but that hardly exculpates him. He took a wild swing at Nancy once and knocked her across the room, though this dramatic result probably was unintentional. Another time he hit her when she was pregnant, which caused him deep remorse once he understood the act's potential consequences.

Images of contempt for and violence against women are plentiful in his writing, which, he acknowledged in *Last Notes from Home,* "frequently evidenced a hatred for women." This borders on understatement. "Slamming your back into the barn-red clapboard, I fervently slapped your face once, then twice, then yet again." "I reared back and with all my might gave Zita a resounding open-handed crack on her left cheek. . . . I had come to see that the one piece of eloquence Zita understood was a fierce boot in the ass." "On the third occasion I grew furious, slapped her face, and tried to get my room key from her." "I read, or glanced at, only those articles about cinema starlets nobody has ever heard of. . . . I used to imagine flogging them to death with a truncheon." "I'd picture John Gentle rising suddenly up out of the perpetual lethargy of his saintlike patience and smacking her right on her nose."

From time to time Fred's writing intimates at least the possibility of tenderness toward women, but those times are rare. Much more characteristic is his approving quotation of a macho friend's boast: "These cunts do what I tell 'em to." What Fred wanted to tell them to do was to get out of his life. He was a misogynist, though the implications of this are anything but simple to detect and understand.

But if one is inclined to believe that Fred's difficulties with conventional society had something to do with repressed or unresolved sexual urges, the same argument can be extended to his misogyny. Homosexual men often get along well with women because, among other reasons, the element of sexual pressure has been eliminated. Is it unreasonable to believe that men of shaky sexual identity who have had sexual experiences only with women, reluctant and unfulfilling ones at that, might well come to hate women? The Watertown culture in which Fred was reared viewed homosexuality as anathema and would have been brutally cruel to any man who showed any sign of it. A man who wanted to be accepted in that culture yet was inherently out of synch with it could have suffered ineradicable hurt, anger and despair; he could have taken this out on women, toward whom he felt harsh resentment and who were easy, vulnerable targets.

It is to this general sense of irreconcilable difference, rather than to the specific possibility of latent, repressed homosexuality, that we most usefully look in Fred Exley's case. His own homophobia was vehement. He knew "the Freudian voodoo, the feelings of inadequacy that sometimes come to a man, the latent homosexuality, and so forth, and even the probable causes for such things," but "it's all hogwash." Though homosexuals are not treated in his books without sympathy, mainly he dismisses them with manly condescension.

Certainly it is possible that Fred was protesting too much in expressing these viewpoints, but that too is a matter of speculation. Fred's sexual persona may or may not have been what he wanted us to believe it was, but this remains a mystery not susceptible to facile solution. In today's social climate, with homosexuality more widely tolerated and with discussion of sexual difference less heated than it was in Fred's day, it is tempting to lay everything at repressed homosexuality and tie it all into a neat, fashionable bundle. Tempting, but the evidence just isn't there.

So, on balance, the possibility of repressed sexual urges is provocative but unanswerable. But the exercise of exploring it is useful, for it underlines the central question of Fred's inherent otherness. He was a misfit, which never is easy, but in his case it was all the harder because the place around which his world revolved was so implacably inhospitable to people who did not fit in. Even if we assume that Fred's sexual tastes were essentially the same as those of most men in his hometown, there remains much more about him that was utterly out of line.

It is revealing that Fred's "wound" and the "rage" with which he bemoaned it do not seem to have become really significant until after Southern California and Chicago. The great discovery he made in those two places was that the life he wanted to live was a life of the mind. He wanted to read and write, and he wanted to occupy his own interior world. He was willing to root for football teams and go out on fishing trips, and to enjoy all of this into the bargain, but such amusements were as peripheral to what really mattered to him as was guy talk at the bar about the looks and sexual conduct of local women.

Making a hard situation all the worse, Fred wanted to be at one with Watertown every bit as much as he wanted to be apart from it. He was as torn as a person could be. When he said that he hated Watertown's narrowness and rigidity and insularity, he meant every word of it. He saw Watertown as America in microcosm; the loathing he at times felt for it arose from exactly the same source as the loathing he at times felt for America. He hated the very idea of the white picket fence and the wife with her apron and the 6:00 A.M. alarm clock.

Yet Fred also meant every word of it when he said that he envied and admired those who were able to make peace with conventional life, to punch their time clocks and to be at dinner promptly at six. He wanted to be unusual, sui generis, but he wanted to be ordinary, too. He was constitutionally incapable of being ordinary, and the world he loved abhorred the unusual. There was no place for him, so he wandered from station to station, finding family and friends who took him in for a while yet always ended up sending him away. He was utterly, irrevocably, on his own. His heartache must have been torture, and his loneliness must have been unbearable.

Fred spent approximately half a year lying on the davenport in the stone house in Pamelia Four Corners. He lived a hermit's life, staring endlessly at the television set and wolfing down Oreo cookies; he claimed that he drank heavily during this period, but he must have sneaked his booze into the house, for Charlotte and Wally did not supply any themselves. Back from Southern California and Chicago and his long homeward journey, Fred knew that in his late twenties he had changed in deep and essential if as yet unidentifiable ways; he was trying to understand and come to terms with the change. He was morose, withdrawn, antisocial. His presence in the house cast a pall over it.

No one was more puzzled and vexed than his stepfather, Wally Richardson. The two men hardly knew each other and had little in common. As a self-made man who had worked with his hands for more than three decades before acquiring his share of a successful manufacturing company, Richardson was accustomed to getting on with the business of life. When he married Charlotte Merkley Exley, he had no way of knowing that a truculent, couch-bound stepson was part of the bargain.

Yet Richardson's forbearance and genuine concern were endless. Not merely was his sofa occupied eternally by a slug, but Fred was deliberately provocative toward him, trying to bait him into confrontations that, in the fantasy world Fred then inhabited, Fred was certain he would win:

> Were he any day going to throw me out onto the street and tell me to go to work, I would have the satisfaction, before he did so, of having confronted him for a long time with a face of unwavering and unmitigated scorn. It never for a moment occurred to me—as it never does to people for whom the world has soured, creating in them the perverse capacity to measure everything and everybody in their own rancid image—that my stepfather had no intention of kicking me out. He was a man of dignity, kindness, and constancy; and, simply stated, he believed in his marriage vows and was accepting me as the "worse" opposed to the "better" the minister had spoken of.

In the late winter and early spring of 1958, Fred did what he later called "an odd thing." He made a private place for himself in the stone house. Rising from his couch, he went upstairs to a twenty- by twenty-foot claustrophobic space above the dining room that Charlotte and Wally used for storage. He could barely stand erect at its center, and its walls sloped sharply to the floor at both sides. The room "was ugly and melancholy, being sprinkled daily with a plaster which made its way through split layers of wallpaper and, falling to the floor in great chunks, detonated, laying a heavy gray fallout over all," yet something about it appealed to Fred. He emptied it of all "the sad, accumulated refuse of my mother's life," stripped its walls and sanded its handsome old pine floor. He refinished secondhand furniture, acquired a typewriter, put his small library in order, and made himself at home. He seems to have known in his bones that he had work to do and that it might be done in this room. But he wasn't ready for that.

Within what had become a hushed household Fred began to hear, "above the unsettling whispers, the words *sick* and *psychiatrist* and *hospital*." His family did not believe Fred was insane, but there was general agreement that his drinking was out of hand and that his moroseness was alarming. When Charlotte failed to persuade him to volunteer for treatment, she asked Irwin Brown, Fran's husband, to try. She knew that Fred respected Irwin's intelligence and would listen to him.

So Irwin climbed the stairs and entered Fred's sanctuary. He closed the door and sat at the end of Fred's bed; Fred was in the chair by the typewriter. "Fred," Irwin said, "this can't go on. It's no good for you, no good for Mom, no good for Wally or the family. We're all in it together." Fred declined to take the bait. "No, I'm all right," he said. "I don't need any help. Don't worry about it."

Obviously he thought about it, though, for shortly thereafter he surrendered. He was taken to Stony Lodge, a private mental institution in Westchester County. As it turned out, Stony Lodge had no answers for Fred. His stay there was brief; he alludes to it only fleetingly in *A Fan's Notes*. Yet Stony Lodge was of great importance in his life, for it was while he was in Westchester that he met Francena Fritz.

She was three years younger than he, the only child of George and Mary Fritz of Beacon, New York. Her father was a figure out of Horatio Alger. Apprenticed as a plumber, he worked hard at his trade and mastered it. He went into business for himself and prospered, becoming a plumbing contractor. He did everything, from installing plumbing to keeping the books. Not infrequently he worked all day with his hands, then returned to the office and did bookkeeping until eleven at night. He and his wife were unpretentious people, responsible and careful with their money. They permitted themselves a Cadillac and a Mercedes, but that was about as much ostentation as they allowed. George Fritz may have been one of the wealthiest men in Beacon, but it was a small, rural town and he lived according to its modest lights.

Francena, who was born in 1932, was the Fritzes' second child; a son had been born earlier but died soon after childbirth. The Fritzes did not spoil Francena, but she was precious to them in much the way that Fred was precious to Charlotte. Busy though he was, her father was always there should Francena need him. She was quiet, shy, pretty, intelligent and sensitive, though occasionally she became extremely extroverted.

Her parents sent Francena to public schools in Beacon and to college at Skidmore, a small private college in Saratoga Springs, then still for women only, with an enviable academic reputation. She did well there and graduated in 1954. She put on no airs; she went right to work in White Plains as a social worker, dealing with children.

When Francena first met Fred Exley, she was singularly unimpressed. Other women were much taken with him—they thought he looked like Clark Gable, sans mustache—but Francena thought he was aloof and didn't like him. He saw something in her, though, and tracked her down after he had left Stony Lodge. They began to court, even though by the fall of 1958 Fred was back in the hospital, at a state institution called Harlem Valley—"Avalon Valley," in *A Fan's Notes*—at Wingdale in Dutchess County near the Connecticut line.

Harlem Valley was "lovely," with "chateau-like houses" and "shrubbed carpet-like lawns [that] ran sweepingly down between ancient, verdant trees." Fred felt immediately at home and put himself in charge. When Fran and Irwin went there and asked for Fred Exley, the attendant said, "Oh, yeah. Hey, Fred!" Fred walked out to greet them as though he were chief administrator, if not king. Everyone from doctors on down deferred to him. But even though he "loved" the place, Fred's days there were hard. Though in retrospect it seems certain that alcohol was his main problem and that enforced abstention from it was the closest anyone could get to a cure, Fred was variously diagnosed as either "paranoiac-schizophrenic" or "schizophrenic-paranoiac," and was subjected to electroshock. He became terrified that lobotomy was next on the list, and in a moment of utter lucidity he determined his course:

> Was I, too, insane? It was a difficult admission to make, but I am glad that I made it; later I came to believe that this admission about oneself may be the only redemption in America. Yes, I was insane. Still, I did not despise my oddness, my deviations, those things which made me, after all, me. I wanted to preserve those things. To do it, I had to get out of that place. Then—as quickly as the rage had come over me—I suddenly knew how to do it. I would be the kind of man I suspected the world wanted me to be.

So Fred, or so at least he later claimed, put on a façade of eager, complaisant normality. He made a briefcase in the hospital's Arts and Crafts Room, and somehow persuaded the staff that this would be his ticket to a normal life on Madison Avenue, even to marriage and family. "I did my job so beautifully that when it came time to leave the hospital I had all but convinced myself that these things were what I thirsted after."

Francena often visited Fred at Harlem Valley, "an attractive girl with roan-colored hair, dressed in a camel's-hair coat, leaning against a steel-gray Mercedes 190 SL convertible." By the fall of 1959 Fred was at large again, and on October 31 of that year he and Francena were married. It was a Sunday, and Halloween to boot. The ceremony was held at the elegant old Hotel Woodruff in Watertown. The presiding official was a local judge; the witnesses were Gordie Phillips and his showgirl of the moment. Francena's parents were not present, but Fred had the bill for the reception sent to them. Somehow a wedding guest ended up in the same bedroom as Fred and Francena that night. He heard Fred shuffling around in the bedclothes, then saw him go to the window and look out at a clock. Fred turned and shouted, "Francena! Francena!" The man heard her stir. "It's twelve o'clock," Fred told her. "I want you to get down on your knees and thank God you got me."

Charlotte knew better. "Fred and Francena are married," she told Bill and Judy. "They came up here and were married at the Woodruff. They didn't come out at all. She wanted to but he wouldn't. She is such a nice girl. It is terrible. I can't imagine what her life will be like and it is terrible but it will take it out of my hands but my heart aches for her."

From the start the marriage was doomed. Any illusions Fred had briefly entertained about normal life immediately vanished. The newlyweds got an apartment in Greenwich, where Francena resumed her career in social work, but Fred was almost never there. From time to time they were happy. Fred read constantly, which gave Francena pleasure, probably because it showed a tantalizing glimpse of a domesticity that never actually materialized. Since he loved to read and didn't want to work, she said, why didn't he write a book?

For a while Fred had a teaching position at Port Chester, but not for long. Most of the time he was either at home with Charlotte in the stone house, or with Gordie Phillips in Albany. He was drunk all the time, and occasionally flew off the handle. Once, not long after their marriage, Francena called Fred's twin sister for help. Fran's father-in-law had just died; Irwin was receiving visitors at the funeral home, but Francena's plea was heart-wrenching. She told Irwin that Fred was throwing things around the house, breaking furniture, threatening to hurt her, hitting her. She didn't know what to do, and begged for help. So Irwin and Fran drove through a storm to Greenwich, where they found everything spotless and serene. They asked Francena where Fred was, and she told him that he had left a while ago, that he was "down in some bar drinking."

On April 29, 1960, Francena gave birth to a daughter, Pamela Rae Exley. No one remembers if Fred was there. He certainly wasn't with Francena often thereafter, and he never gave any indication that fatherhood interested him in the least. The marriage was a couple of years old when George Fritz finally decided that he could not permit his daughter and granddaughter to be subject to Fred's whims, indignities and indifference. He offered Francena a deal: if she would agree to divorce Fred, he would buy her a house in Greenwich. This saddened Francena, but her father was persistent and she was realistic enough to understand what lay ahead of her. In 1962 she flew to Mexico and obtained a quickie divorce.

Francena and Pamela moved into the house, a comfortable but modest structure in one of Greenwich's unglamorous neighborhoods. Francena continued to do social work, and undertook postgraduate study in order to improve her qualifications, first at Columbia and then at the University of Hawaii, obtaining a master's degree at the latter. George Fritz helped with some of her expenses, but for the most part she was on her own. She and Pamela lived ordered and fruitful lives. Pamela grew into an uncommonly pretty girl who, apart from a yearning for stability and a wariness of alcohol, showed little evidence of the disarray into which her parents' marriage had fallen so early.

It probably didn't hurt that Fred was hardly ever around, for his presence would have been more disruptive than useful. He was in Watertown when the marriage broke up. From 1962 until the publication of *A Fan's Notes* in September 1968, he drifted from upstate New York, where he held occasional teaching jobs in small towns like Clayton and Gouverneur, to Florida, where he sponged off Charlotte and Wally when they were on vacation, and back to Harlem Valley, where he had one final stay. He spoke to Pamela by telephone from time to time, and dropped by the house even more rarely. Once at Easter he brought her a chocolate rabbit, and when she was older he offered paternal, or avuncular, advice about college and career and other adult matters about which he seemed, inexplicably, to regard himself as an expert. When she was eighteen and developing an interest in art, he urged her to consider the Parsons School of Design, and later he pressed the University of Iowa upon her. But these bursts of attention were sporadic. As *A Fan's Notes* was on the verge of publication he claimed in a letter to Francena that the book originally had been dedicated to Pamela but that "my now-also-ex wife threw a fit . . . , saying that she'd never really be my daughter, etc. etc., and to keep peace I took the easy way and substituted her name, which is all the bitch really wanted anyway." There is no evidence elsewhere to substantiate this self-serving claim.

Fred was as unhelpful about his daughter's financial needs as he was about her emotional ones. In April 1975 Francena obtained a support order against him from family court in Jefferson County. He was supposed to pay her fifty dollars a month beginning the following month, but failed to do so. This set off a brief flurry of legal activity in the course of which a probation officer said that "Mr. Exley has been in the hospital and is unable to work at present." His "outstanding bills" came to a total of $4,625.35 and he "is asking to have [Francena] exonerate support payments until February 1, 1977 until he gets back on his feet." Never having been on his feet to begin with, Fred was in a perfect position to evade his responsibilities into the foreseeable future, which is precisely what he did, at times in a mood of self-righteousness. In August 1978 he wrote to his probation officer:

Attorney Jack Scordo said I should apprise you of my present finances. After I pay my August rent, which I haven't yet paid, and last month's phone bill, I estimate that I will have the enormous sum of $3.58 in my savings account. This figure does not include my present indebtedness. In fact, I am doubtless going to have to sell my studio to my landlord, furniture, books, etc., in order to stay alive.

I told Mrs. Exley of my plight, she later told me she had written you and asked you to relieve me of my payments until that time I was unable to pay and said she had received a letter back informing her that it was up to the court to determine whether or not I could pay. However, Mr. Scordo informs me that you have no such letter in your files. I don't know if this is one of my ex-wife's stories, but I can hardly believe that she'd pull this nonsense on me.

Fred sent a copy of this letter to Francena and scrawled a note to her on it: "If you lied to me, I'll never again lift a finger to help Pamela, with jobs or anything. These bastards are talking about arresting me!" It is something of a miracle that a year later he managed to come up with five hundred dollars, which he sent to Pamela, who had matriculated at the State University of New York at Purchase. She needed a car to get back and forth between home and school. Fred magnanimously donated this vast sum toward "some kind of car." He claimed full credit for his generosity. He had told Francena in advance of the gift that "I said I'd do my damndest to get Pamela the $500 for a car, and I will *absolutely do my damndest* before she returns to school in the fall," and when he sent the check he made a point of telling Pamela that "as per usual I'm broke but I do have a subletter in my apartment, so I will stay with my mother."

The torch that Francena carried for Fred never burned out. In 1980 she got New York State automobile plates that read "EXLEY.1." A year later she was even willing to consider letting him resume living with her in Greenwich, though she objected that she would become his "sole financial benefactor." She told him she loved him and that she probably always would, but she was as exasperated by him as was everyone else. She wanted him to stop wasting his talents on being a con artist. She suspected, correctly, that he had a real fear of relationships with anyone, especially women. He was in Florida, where she was sure he could find work of some sort—picking oranges part-time, if nothing else—so as to help support himself. But however irritated she may have been, she urged him to take care of himself and to write to her, and she signed off, "Love, Francena."

She was devoted to Fred right to the end. At his memorial service in 1992 she told a reporter for the *Watertown Daily Times,* "In his own way, as bad as he was and as much carousing as he did, he was very old fashioned about family and other institutions. He just couldn't take responsibility like a lot of other people do or have to. But he was an extremely intelligent and interesting person. He was a wonderful person." He was, she said, "the love of my life." She was one of the best people who entered his life, but he was no more capable of sustaining a connection with her than he was with anyone else.

At some level he knew what he had missed, or thrown away. In *A Fan's Notes* his portrait of Francena, whom he calls Patience, is admiring and affectionate. Her "taste in clothes and food and furniture seemed to me flawless." She had "an admirably feminine diffidence and a true bounteousness of spirit." He was "aware of the dignity you were affording my shabby humanity," but he was incapable of repaying it. That he had married Francena in the first place is as much a mystery as anything else he ever did. He had no gift for domesticity or fidelity—he once ranked himself as a marriage prospect, on a scale of one hundred, "about seven and a half, somewhere around my I.Q."—and absolutely no sense of obligation to anyone else. Yet five years after the end of his first marriage he was into another, equally ill-fated. When *that* wife said farewell he was heard to say, "Shit, now I'll have to find another one," but to some woman's everlasting mercy, he never followed through.

With Francena's Mexican divorce in hand, Fred was free once again, though any implication that he was anything but free as a bird during the marriage should not be taken seriously. He went back to Mom and was taken in as usual without question or objection. How Charlotte felt about the end of his marriage is not recorded, but it is safe to assume that she was both confirmed in her initial apprehension and sorry for Francena and Pamela. From time to time Francena phoned her, but the connection between the two of them was tenuous and was eventually severed. Pamela, to her deep regret, never got to know her grandmother; by the time she established a rapprochement with Fred, in the 1990s, Charlotte was dead.

But Charlotte never let her disapproval of Fred's actions color her everlasting, unquestioning loyalty to him. Wally, who had paid for Fred's initial hospitalization at Stony Lodge and had underwritten him in innumerable other ways, stood ready as usual to assist in any way he could. The two had found peace with each other several years before, and had struck up a friendship based on Fred's growing respect for Wally's strength and his willingness to assume responsibility for others, on Wally's devotion to Charlotte and all the children she brought with her to their marriage, and on a shared affection for the New York Giants. One afternoon in 1967, seated before the television set "at that high and exhilarating moment just prior to the kickoff," Wally "closed his eyes, slid silently to the floor, and died painlessly of a coronary occlusion."

It was a terrible loss for Charlotte, not merely because she had lost her husband but because his legacy was small; for the rest of her life her financial condition was perilous. Fred was deeply saddened too, but at least had the consolation of knowing that, as had not been the case between him and Earl Exley, he had reached an accommodation with Wally Richardson that pleased both men. It is a pity that Wally did not live a bit longer, for he would have been as proud—and doubtless as surprised—as any born Exley. All those years of lying on the davenport, of disappearing into the room upstairs, of seeking direction and discipline at Harlem Valley, were soon to bear fruit. The unexpected child, the wonder boy, was about to do something so unexpected, so wonderful, that he would leave all who knew him dumbfounded and amazed. Fred Exley was about to become an author.

PART TWO

HIS
ROYAL
FREDNESS

Fred signing *A Fan's Notes* in Watertown, 1968
Watertown Daily Times

IN THE MORGUE OF THE *WATERTOWN DAILY TIMES* IS A seven-line memorandum on a fading, fragile sheet of cheap copy paper such as newspapers used in the days of typewriters and linotype machines. Dated January 24, 1966, it reads: "Fred Exley is in Florida with his mother and stepfather. At one time he taught school at Indian River. Once he wrote a book on 'Footnotes of North Country', but publishers turned it down, saying it was libelous. He was asked to rewrite it. Whether he did and submitted it again to the publishers is not known."

That document is positively runic, filled as it is with meanings and implications far transcending its offhand brevity. It reminds us that nearly four decades after Fred's birth, Watertown was still small enough so that the doings of its every resident were of interest and import to the local newspaper, down to and including those of a ne'er-do-well who had thus far managed to achieve little more distinction than that of minor local character; that Fred was still spong-

ing off Charlotte and Wally but now had taken this operation to Florida; that such employment as he had found
locally was in teaching.

It also tells us that the publishing history of *A Fan's Notes*
dates back to a time before its acceptance by Harper & Row.
There can be no question that "Footnotes of North Country," or whatever the manuscript actually was called, is *A
Fan's Notes* in some phase of its gestation. The claim that it
was libelous rings true, for fragmentary evidence indicates
that *A Fan's Notes* was written as a memoir and then revised
as a novel—or at least the names and some of the places
were changed—because editors and lawyers feared action
by some of those named in it. If anything, it is probable that
the manuscript to which this memorandum refers bore a
considerable resemblance to the finished book, for by this
time the essential shape and specific details of his story seem
to have become quite clear in Fred's mind.

How *A Fan's Notes* came to be written is not, as it turns
out, a question that this biography can answer. If Fred
saved his early drafts, eventually he disposed of them in one
fashion or another; the full manuscript of *A Fan's Notes*
now at the University of Rochester is so pristine as to yield
few useful clues. The files of Fred's literary agency and
publisher are empty; it is odd—no, infuriating—that institutions that profit from literature do not always trouble
themselves to preserve evidence documenting how it gets
made, but it is inescapable reality. As to the memories of
those who were present at the creation, they have been
dimmed by time and, more to the point, few of those who
were around when *A Fan's Notes* was working its way
through Fred's notepads and typewriter had the slightest
idea what was taking place.

Some of these people, most of them Watertown family and friends who had known Fred all his life, were aware that something was going on, but none of them took it seriously: That's Freddie, they said, up in the attic fiddling the time away. If anything he did was taken seriously by anyone, this was his teaching, which at least provided intermittent proof that he was not wholly incapable of supporting himself and, by no means incidentally, was a respectable middle-class occupation. Over time, by his own testimony, Fred spent a total of seven years as a schoolteacher, mostly of high school English and mostly in places within shouting distance of Watertown.

"I'd never be a teacher," Fred wrote. "I had neither the patience nor the wit nor the wherewithal to give students less than I knew; worse, whatever intelligence I possessed was of that savagely unsympathetic kind which didn't allow me to understand the student's difficulty in grasping: sadly, I lacked the intelligence to simplify, and with an utterly monolithic and formidable pedantry I thought nothing of demanding that my students feed me back my own quackery." For once in his life Fred underestimated himself. Though most students either ignored him or dismissed him, a few were attracted and even inspired by his passion. In these rural classrooms, and later at the University of Iowa, Fred acquired a handful of acolytes, students who were stimulated by his teaching and who stayed in touch with him for years. He may have had no patience for the drab routine of a curriculum drawn up by drones, but he had the innate urge of the born teacher, the irresistible desire to spread his own message; that he did so more effectively in a book than in a classroom should not permit us to dismiss out of hand his performance in the latter.

In contrast with his teaching jobs, Fred's other gainful employment during the early 1960s was a joke. In May 1961, soon after his return to the stone house, Fred was given a provisional appointment as clerk and crier of the supreme and county courts in Jefferson County. Unlike his immediate predecessor in that job, Robert V. Renzi, brother of Fred's high school teammate Eugene Renzi, Fred was not a lawyer and had no expectation of ever becoming one. The job was just another way of making a few dollars and, like all his other jobs, it did not last long; but the picture of Fred Exley, who despised procedure and rigmarole, acting as an administrator of legal routine is absolutely delicious.

All this marginal employment was the conventional face that Fred presented to the world. Behind it, unknown to anyone in its full dimensions, was the writing he was doing. Fred wrote not, as most who knew about it assumed, for whatever might be his private pleasure, but out of a deep conviction that in time his work would be published and would find readers. If Fred seemed unsurprised when his book achieved its improbable success, it was because he believed that this, like everything else that came to him over the years, was his proper due, his entitlement.

Exley family mythology has it that *A Fan's Notes* was written upstairs behind that closed door in the stone house. There is some truth to this, but no one still alive ever heard the sound of a typewriter in that building. Occasionally family members sneaked glimpses at the manuscript, but no one got reports on work in progress. Memories of the process of creation in that house are in large measure the offspring of hindsight. At the time most people thought that Fred was either ineffectual or lazy, and that his occasional allusions to his writing were just a way of saying, "Well, I'm an author," of ascribing an identity to himself that he had not earned. People also knew that he was writing about his own life, so when the book actually materialized, many of them just shrugged it off; that's easy, they said, writing about yourself.

As it turns out, the best source for the origins of *A Fan's Notes* is *A Fan's Notes*. During his first stay at Harlem Valley, in the 1960s, Fred came under the care of a friendly, sympathetic doctor. This "Dr. K." found a make-work job for Fred, checking on whether other patients were showing up for their own make-work jobs, and arranged a private room for him, "a highly coveted possession," where he was allowed to write: "Not that Dr. K. necessarily believed I was a writer. Still, he seemed to understand that trying to break and adjust people to what may be an inhuman society is an unwarranted undertaking and that rebellion, in whatever form, is not always an unhealthy enterprise." So Fred began, "started fearfully into the past in search of answers" to what it was in him that had brought him to that hospital:

> In many ways that book was this book, which I wasn't then ready to write. Without a thought of organization I wrote vignettes and thirty-page paragraphs about anything and everything I could remember. There are times now when, in nostalgia, I tell myself I'll never again put down the things I did then, but I know I'm only confusing quantity with quality. If nothing else, I wrote a great deal during those months, writing rapidly, furiously, exultantly, heart-sinkingly, and a manuscript of whatever merit began, page by page, filling up the suitcase at the foot of my iron cot.

Harlem Valley gave Fred two things that were absolutely essential to the writing of his book: discipline and sobriety.

He could not fritter away his time in bars and he could not deaden his memory or imagination with alcohol. He says that what he wrote in the hospital was primarily disorganized bits and pieces, hurled onto the page with anger and urgency as he recalled "the horror and the dismay, the laughter and the bitterness, of that holocaust I called my life." This is plausible, for Fred was an untutored writer and a man in a state of emotional torment. The former needed an apprenticeship and the latter needed to be harnessed. That Fred was able to act as his own mentor is quite extraordinary, but it seems to be true. No one has come forward to claim credit for shaping him, and Fred himself gave no such credit to anyone. He was his own teacher and his own editor, living proof that the best way to learn to write well is to read well and to practice, practice, practice.

Precisely what Fred brought home to the stone house from Harlem Valley we cannot know, but the person who was closest to him as *A Fan's Notes* headed into the home-stretch—his second wife, Nancy Glenn—believes that "he was sitting up in his room on a finished manuscript." She should know, because it was in large measure because of what became *A Fan's Notes* that she fell in love with him. Their marriage was brief and unhappy and tempestuous. Because it coincided with the completion and publication of *A Fan's Notes,* its story must be told now.

Nancy Glenn was twenty years old when she met Fred Exley; he was thirty-six. She was the elder of two daughters of an upper-middle-class couple whose marriage was loveless and nomadic. Her father was an engineer whose work took him around the world, leaving Nancy with little sense of roots or home. She attended a Quaker boarding school in Ohio and then, for only a year, the College of Charleston, in the South Carolina city that was her mother's hometown. While there she met an older man who was nice to her, who gave her the attention and affection she craved, who stood ready to take her away from the barren ground of her own household. So she married him in 1965 and moved with him to Palm Beach Shores, on the Atlantic coast of Florida not far north of Miami and Fort Lauderdale, where he bought a yacht club and resort called the Buccaneer.

Nancy was still under legal age, so she couldn't work in the Buccaneer's bar. Instead she ran the switchboard, participated in redecorating, met and greeted guests, and otherwise tried to make herself useful. She was good-looking, dark-haired, sexy, well dressed: an ornament for her husband, toward whom she felt gratitude and fondness, but neither passion nor love. Theirs was a quiet marriage.

One day as she walked through the dining room, which adjoined the bar, she heard the usual chatter of the usual beach bums who hung out there. An endless stream of profanity, fuckin' this and fuckin' that, issued forth from a guy at the bar. She learned that his name was Fred Exley, but nothing about him interested her. The guys all called him "Ex" and clearly looked up to him in some way, but she found him physically unappealing and was put off by his language and his unchanging state of inebriation.

Then all of a sudden she found herself alone in the same room with him. Her husband had had to fire the bookkeeper because he was a drunk and, in an impulsive decision such as leaves one wondering about the inner workings of the human mind, had hired Fred in his stead. So there they were in the club's little office, Nancy at the switchboard and Fred at the desk. Someone found out about this and said to her, "Oh, he's the writer. He's writing a book." She could only imagine that it was pornography.

Still, they were together in close quarters. Fred made remarks that Nancy thought were sexist and otherwise offended her, but over time their casual chitchat took on a warmer tone. He let it be known that he had something that needed to be typed; he could type, he said, but didn't have a typewriter. She said she'd be willing to do the job for him. As she got deeper and deeper into it, she found herself thinking: My God! I can't believe it! Coming out of *this* guy! It was a long passage about an aluminum-siding salesman whom Fred called Mr. Blue, and its sensitivity brought Nancy up short.

That sensitive side of Fred is what she fell in love with, but it didn't happen overnight. They talked from time to time about what he was writing—she was one of the few people to whom Fred extended this privilege—and she came to see him in a sympathetic light. Most days he was reasonably sober, and his voice even achieved occasional animation; he was primarily interested in talking about himself, but his self-absorption had not yet reached its full mature dimensions. They became friends. Nancy cooked a few meals for him, which gave her pleasure because all her own came from the club's restaurant; she did the cooking in her apartment and brought the food to the office for Fred.

They fell into the habit of taking walks on Jupiter Beach, a few miles up the coast. Their relationship was still platonic, but things to come can be detected in their recourse to a place beyond Nancy's husband's reach. Fred talked to her a lot on the beach about Watertown and his war years, as he described them. He said that he had been injured in Korea, which explained his slightly crooked right arm, and that a bullet had ricocheted off his head. Not until much later did she realize that he was wrapping himself in his brother Bill's story, a fabrication that had much to do with her parents' implacable hostility to him.

A long time passed, over the course of which Nancy fell deeply in love with Fred, to the point of worshiping him. When he wasn't drinking he seemed to her a dear spirit, infantile and helpless; he used to tell her that "we're all afraid of everything," that "we're all scared to death." Like others who knew him, she was willing to let the drinking pass in the hope that the other side was the real Fred Exley. At last she left her husband and took her own apartment in Palm Beach Shores, and she and Fred became lovers. Until then he had never made any moves on her, and after they ended up in bed together he stewed over the impropriety of it all: "*This* can't go on and we can't do *this* right under your husband's nose." Long after they had parted she looked back with affection on this oddly conventional side of him, which she attributed to Charlotte's influence.

During this phase Fred and Nancy lived together in her apartment only intermittently. He stayed with Charlotte and Wally when they came down on vacation, and in his own mysterious places, but in time he and Nancy found quarters at Jupiter. He got a job at the *Palm Beach Post*'s copy desk, then walked away from it when his inner siren called him back to Watertown in the summer of 1967. Nancy was working as a receptionist in the beauty department of Burdine's department store, but had to quit because she was ill so often. She went home to Charleston, where her mother took her to a doctor. When Fred telephoned that night, she told him she was pregnant.

"Put your mother on the phone," he told her, and when her mother got on the line, he said, "Send Nancy north."

"She's not going anywhere," was the reply, "she's staying here."

"Well," said Fred, "if you don't send her north, I'm coming down there and I'm going to let that whole fuckin' town of Charleston know that she's pregnant."

Nancy went north. She moved into the stone house, where she immediately became infatuated with Charlotte and Wally, both of whom treated her tenderly. Fred was another matter. His dark side had begun to assert itself. In Florida there had been a few ugly scenes—he spat in her food and threw drinks at her—but in the stone house things got worse. He grabbed her, shook her, shoved her up against walls, but it didn't really matter because her own childhood had taught her that pain equals love. She loved Fred, she didn't consider the idea of abortion, which at the time was still uncommon and unsafe, and she put up with the wild swings in his mood; one day he was filled with utter hatred for her, and the next he smothered her in an all-consuming love. She knew that his rage arose from a belief that life is painful, that rage was one of the ways pain expressed itself, and she put up with it.

When Nancy first got to the stone house, Fred slept in her room, but after a couple of nights he moved out and locked himself in his own room under the sloping roof. His rage was building. He had been stealing drinking funds from Charlotte and Wally. Wallets and purses had been hidden from him. Fred didn't have money, he didn't have a car, they wouldn't let him keep booze in the house. One night he came down, found the keys to Wally's car, and hit the highway. By the time he got back his departure had been discovered and everyone was waiting up for him. He was drunk out of his mind. He staggered to the back porch, emitting a stream of profanity along the way, and grabbed a gallon of blue paint. He heaved the paint against the wall; in moments the entire porch was splattered with blue. "I hate all of you cocksuckers!" he shouted. "I'm getting out of here!"

He left, but he came back. On September 13, 1967, he and Nancy were married, and on January 12, 1968, their daughter, Alexandra, was born. Fred was at the hospital, took one look at his child—"She doesn't look a thing like me," he said—and left. That was the beginning of the end; her husband's utter lack of interest in his daughter, more than anything else he had done to her previously, was what convinced Nancy that the marriage was hopeless. When she and the baby got home to their little apartment in Watertown, Fred did a bit of perfunctory oohing and aahing, but diapers and other parental duties were beyond his interest or competence. This strengthened her determination to escape from the marriage.

In June, Nancy went back to Charleston. Fred dropped her and the baby off at her mother's house—he wasn't permitted to come in—and then drove to Florida, expecting that she would soon join him. When he learned that she had no intention of doing so, he hit the roof. Disbelief came first, then anger. But Nancy was adamant. She stayed in Charleston, and eventually got involved with a wealthy upstate New York businessman. He was attentive and generous, and the needs that had nagged at her all her life were as urgent as ever. He put her and Alex up in a luxurious apartment house in Syracuse and took good care of her. Still, Nancy's feelings about Fred included love as well as anger and hurt, and she hadn't made a full break. So when she learned that Fred would be signing copies of *A Fan's Notes* at Robinson's Book Store in Watertown in early October, she packed Alex in the car her lover had turned over to her and went up to be a part of the excitement, bringing an unabridged dictionary as her gift to the new author.

It was a happy reunion. Nancy and Fred spent what she recalled as a "wonderful, glorious" night together. But John O'Neill, Connie's husband, figured out that the car Nancy was driving belonged to her lover's company fleet; he asked her what was going on. There was an unpleasant confrontation in which Fred actually stood up for Nancy. He put her and the child in the company car, dropped it off at the airport, and took them to Syracuse. He moved in, her businessman stopped paying rent, and they were on their own again.

The incident had lasting repercussions within the Exley family. Fred's siblings had been suspicious of Nancy from the outset. This grew deeper when she refused to go to Florida with Fred, and became more rigid when rumors about her extramarital involvement made their way through the Watertown gossip mill. The last straw was her unannounced arrival at Fred's book signing; Fred's family thought she was trying to jump on the bandwagon now that he was a published author of modest renown. Whether justified or not, these suspicions and ill feelings persisted over the years.

Fred stayed with Nancy and Alex in Syracuse for about half a year. Stayed, that is, in his fashion. Between Christmas and New Year's he left one day for a quart of milk—in this case the proverbial story is literally true—and didn't come home for two weeks; he called on New Year's Eve from New York City. Nancy was pregnant, with a child whom she readily acknowledged was not Fred's, but he stood by her, though his physical abuse of her did not stop.

When her son was born in April 1969 with terrible defects that eventually killed him, Fred was stricken with remorse. "I'll never forgive myself for what I did," he said over and over. Nancy tried to explain that she had had toxoplasmosis, an infection that has much the same effects upon pregnancy as German measles, but Fred could not be placated.

Soon Fred left, as he always did. He and Nancy had seen a marriage counselor, who had told them they should seek further guidance and should not divorce, but matters between them grew ever more acrimonious. The lawyers assumed their customary places, and legal proceedings began. On January 8, 1971, a divorce order was issued by the State Supreme Court of New York in Syracuse; the decree told, in depressing detail, the chronicle of a marriage gone bad. Fred was ordered to pay one hundred dollars a week for support of Nancy and Alex. He never paid a cent.

It is a measure of the hold Fred could exert on people that neither Nancy nor Alex ever fully let go of him. Nancy remarried in 1972, to a physicist with Texas Instruments, and moved to Dallas. Fred slipped out of their lives, but late in that decade he came to town to do interviews for a magazine piece that involved the Dallas Cowboys professional football team. He called and invited Nancy and Alex out to dinner. Nancy was hesitant, because she had a new life and a new husband and had no expectation that Fred would ever be a proper father to her daughter. With her husband's blessings she finally decided to accept. Fred showed up a day late, but the dinner went well. He teased Alex in a way that delighted her, and showered her with souvenirs he'd cadged from the Cowboys.

Thus began a long courtship between father and daughter that at times had happy consequences for both of them; the rest of this tale belongs at a later time in Fred's life. As for Nancy, her third marriage ended as her first and second had, but she continued her life with greater purpose and self-assurance. She went to North Texas State and got a degree in anthropology, but was sick of hot, flat country and moved back to New York. During the summer of 1985 she stayed with Charlotte for several weeks, in the little house at 77 Walton Street in Alexandria Bay that Charlotte had bought and moved into after Wally's death. Subsequently Nancy purchased a four-acre lot with an old farmhouse in Cuyler, twenty-five miles south of Syracuse; she planted a large herb garden and opened her own small business, selling dried herbs, herbal vinegar and other goods. She didn't see all that much of Fred, but it pleased her that he and Alex had become close. Every once in a while her phone rang—usually at two or three in the morning—and there was Fred, droning away. She knew that he needed an audience and that hers was just another number to dial, but they had a shared past that was important to her, and listening to his monologues was a small price to pay for the happy memories, which in time became more important than the sad ones.

By the time Nancy and Fred got married, *A Fan's Notes* was only a year away from publication. The manuscript first surfaced for objective readership in 1964, when Fred sent it to David B. Harris, managing editor of Houghton Mifflin Company in Boston, with whom he had crossed paths occasionally when both were students at Watertown High School in the early 1940s. Even for one so blissfully assured of his ultimate literary triumph as Fred was, placing the manuscript in alien hands must have been reason for apprehension, all the more so since it was going out not with an agent's imprimatur but, in publishing jargon, "over the transom." That he chose a fellow son of Watertown suggests that he wanted its first reader to be someone who knew the world about which he wrote, someone who would not dismiss the book out of hand.

It was a lucky choice. Houghton Mifflin did not accept the book, but its editors "felt at the time that he displayed quite a bit of talent," Harris told the *Watertown Daily Times* in 1968, as well as "the ability to handle a range of emotions in a precise way that is the hallmark of a great writer." Harris returned the manuscript with a letter full of praise in which suggestions for its revision were offered. "The book is openly autobiographical in some ways," Harris later recalled, "and I was impressed with the vitality of the writing. The hero suffers pain, and this really comes across."

In contrast with the indifference in other places to documents tracking Fred's literary history, what Houghton Mifflin gave Fred was publishing at its best: the full, heartfelt encouragement of a reputable house with a long, distinguished history. Fred would end up with another such house when Harper & Row accepted *A Fan's Notes* for publication, but Harris's words must have been just the tonic he needed to plunge back into his disorderly creation. That Houghton Mifflin ultimately did not accept the book is far less important than the boost it gave Fred at a time when one was badly needed. To whatever extent Fred was capable of gratitude, he must have been grateful for that.

Another person who saw the book at this early stage was Joe Fox, an editor at Random House. He did not take the book, but he told Fred it "was much too good to be circulating without an agent," and referred him to Lynn Nesbit at the Sterling Lord literary agency. By the late 1990s Nesbit had become one of the most prominent and successful agents in New York, full partner with Morton Janklow in a firm that represented famous writers for whom it negotiated hugely lucrative contracts. In the mid-1960s, though, she was just another of those bright young women who leave college each year and head for Manhattan with dreams of books and authors in their heads.

She had graduated from Northwestern University in 1960, having majored in Oral Interpretation of Literature in the drama school; this gave her a keen appreciation for an author's voice and eventually enabled her to represent some of the most distinctive writers of her day, not merely Fred but also Hunter Thompson, Donald Barthelme and Tom Wolfe. She attended the summer publishing course at Radcliffe, an intensive program that is an open sesame, albeit an expensive one, to jobs in and about publishing. For a couple of months after that she worked as an editorial apprentice at the *Ladies' Home Journal,* but while at Radcliffe she had met the literary agent Sterling Lord, who presided over a session and who ended up offering her a job as all-around gofer in his small office. She was mail clerk, file clerk, receptionist and everything else that was too menial for Lord or the other agent in the firm.

Lord's clients, then as now, tended to the journalistic rather than the literary. Lynn's chief interest, by contrast, was in literature, so when the manuscript of a novel or a collection of short stories found its way to the agency it often ended up on her desk. Her first break occurred when she discovered *Big Broadcast of 1938,* by Barthelme. She took it on, and him, and with that her career was under way. She was all of twenty-two or twenty-three years old.

Not long thereafter, Fred Exley came into her life. Lynn had absolutely no interest in sports, but Fred's voice grabbed her and would not let her go. He had, she remembered, "an incredible combination of irony, humor, self-pity and laser-beam intelligence." She responded powerfully to his pain and to his ability to elevate himself above it with self-deprecation and irony. Sometime in 1964 she agreed to represent him.

For the rest of Fred's life, Lynn was one of the most important people in it. He relied on her absolutely and, with only occasional exceptions, unquestioningly. Though her manner was efficient and purposeful, she responded to his "sweetness," his "vulnerability" and his "fragility" in ways that left no doubt she cared about him very much. Like everyone else in his life she finally got more of his telephone calls than she wanted, and she irritated him when she declined to represent him for relatively unremunerative magazine and newspaper assignments as well as for books, but there were many times when she was at the absolute center of his existence. Talking with friends and literary folk, he rambled on about "Lynn says . . ." and "Lynn tells me . . ." and "Lynn thinks . . ." So far as he was concerned hers was the voice of authority on all matters involving literature and commerce. With one brief exception—he got sore for a while and took his nonexistent business to Elaine Markson—he stuck with Lynn as she moved from Sterling Lord to International Famous Agency to Janklow & Nesbit. Their relationship was strictly business on one level and strictly platonic on another, but in his way he loved her.

Lynn started shopping his manuscript around soon after taking Fred on, but for a long time his prospects looked bleak. A dozen publishers looked at it, a dozen turned it down. A number took it seriously and spoke admiringly about it, but decided against publication. Others responded similarly: the author was talented but unknown; a book that seemed to be about football would have trouble getting the reviews it needed and finding a literary readership; the language was unpleasant; there were potential problems involving libel. At the time the book came out, Fred claimed that Viking originally had bought it, "but I had a conflict over what should come out of the book and what should stay in so I returned the Viking advance of $500."

At last the manuscript landed at the right place, the desk of David Segal at Harper & Row. He was a man of average height but immense appetite, for food and drink and words. In his late thirties, Segal was in his third publishing job; he had previously worked at McGraw-Hill and New American Library. His passion for literature was as insatiable as Fred's, and he responded to the manuscript Lynn sent him with just the enthusiasm and excitement Fred craved. He took the book quickly, for an advance of three thousand dollars. It was unfinished, but his confidence in it was great, and this buoyed Fred incalculably as he went about the task of completing it.

Segal's literary tastes were catholic, but his great love was the literary avant-garde. The most notable author apart from Fred whom he discovered and promoted was William H. Gass, whose remarkable first novel, *Omensetter's Luck,* Segal published in 1966. On the whole he was more effective with literary authors than with commercial publishing. He was in the business not to make money, for himself or anyone else, but to advance the cause of authors and books he believed in. He was not a flamboyant person, but he had a flamboyant style. In the days when the three-martini lunch was still commonplace, Segal drank four or five, or more. He had his own table at La Côte Basque when it was the hottest restaurant in Manhattan, and at the Four Seasons long before it became publishing's most desirable lunching spot. His expense account was staggering, so much so that Harper was relieved when he decided, in 1970, to take it and himself to Knopf.

Fred had little in common with many of Segal's authors and was not especially attuned to their work. Whatever license he may have granted himself—not to mention abused—in obscenity and scatology, he was at heart an old-fashioned writer who worshiped at the shrines of story, character development and sense of place. He loved the work of Vladimir Nabokov, but had little sympathy for younger writers who picked up Nabokov's word play while ignoring his humanity. It was Segal's enthusiasm for the writing of Fred Exley to which Fred most positively responded, not Segal's personal literary tastes.

But that enthusiasm was more than enough. Fred loved David Segal as he loved Lynn Nesbit, in the same way and for the same reason. Here was another smart, sophisticated person, well versed in publishing and its ways, who had taken Fred under his wing and promised him unstinting support. Little else though the two men had in common, they certainly had that.

That Segal was Jewish is noteworthy for two reasons. The first is that in the mid-1960s Jews were at last beginning to break down the prejudices that had kept them out of the "gentleman's business" of book publishing. Doors had been opened in the 1920s by Bennett Cerf at Random House, as well as by Horace Liveright and Alfred A. Knopf at their own firms, but as late as 1960 few others had been able to pass through them. When Mel Zerman joined the Harper sales department in 1959, the number of Jews in that big old house could be counted on the fingers of his hands. By the time Segal arrived a few years later more Jews were employed by the firm, but their numbers were still small and being Jewish was something that people in the business still remarked upon.

The second reason is that Segal was one of four Jews whose roles in Fred's life were important and whose friendship he treasured. The others were Zerman, Jerry Raskin and David Markson. This would not be a matter for comment except that Fred grew up in an isolated part of the world where prejudices against the alien and unknown were virulent. Precisely to what degree Fred himself shared these prejudices is unclear. On the one hand he represented himself as friendly to blacks and other minorities, yet on the other hand he was fully capable of disagreeable language that suggested disagreeable thoughts. "Spades," "spics" and "fags" were terms he did not hesitate to use, at least when talking or writing to those whom he doubted would be offended by them, not to mention the highly derogatory words he routinely used in describing women. As with women, he often used these terms in a humorous, or calculatedly outrageous, way; he loved to be the bad little boy, so it isn't always easy to tell when he was kidding, when he was not. Yet Zerman, Raskin and Markson sensed no anti-Semitic prejudice in him, so we must assume that Segal would have testified similarly.

If Segal played any significant editorial role in *A Fan's Notes* apart from signing it up and promoting it zealously, no hint of it remains. So far as can be determined, the book that the world knows is the book Fred wrote, edited and revised by no one but himself. Segal did come to Watertown to see Fred before the book was published, but this seems to have been more in the way of moral support than of editorial revision; either he or Harper's lawyers insisted on changes in the manuscript that would make it a "fictional memoir" rather than a memoir pure and simple, but this was a legal rather than an editorial decision.

Segal stayed with Fred and Nancy in their apartment upstairs in a house on Flower Avenue. It was an odd encounter. The two men obviously admired and liked each other, yet they had almost nothing in common. At dinner they and Nancy sat in complete silence, a vague sense of discomfort hovering over them. There was no bantering back and forth, no literary gossip, no weighty conversation. Segal came to town, picked up his manuscript, boosted his author's self-confidence by some mysterious means, and headed back to Manhattan.

Whatever his exact relationship with Fred, Segal was wholehearted in his support for Fred's book. He strongly believed that it could reach more than a literary readership and was determined to bring this about. However unsuccessful he may have been previously at pushing his books inside the house, in Fred's behalf he was energetic and effective. He was convinced that the book would be awarded the Harper Prize, an in-house award for fiction carrying a purse of fifteen thousand dollars and considerable prestige; he delayed publication of the book for about a year in expectation of this windfall, but was disappointed. Thereafter he made the sales division his first priority and won its full blessing, in substantial measure because Mel Zerman was passionate about the book. Someone in sales had the idea of printing a specially bound advance copy of the novel for booksellers, a common practice today but rare at the time, especially for a literary book. This was done—the few surviving copies now fetch a handsome price on the infrequent occasions when they reach the marketplace—and to useful effect. In the customary crowd of first novels, *A Fan's Notes* stood out.

By this time *A Fan's Notes* had finally made its way through the Exley family. One day Fred showed up at his twin sister's house with a manuscript in hand. He gave it to his brother-in-law: "Irwin, read this." Irwin read it at night in bed, with amazement washing over him. The version he read was in rough form, with many misspellings. He later asked Fred if he wanted him to proofread the manuscript, but Fred said, "No, it's going to get a professional proofreading." Irwin's only negative comment was that he didn't like the abrupt changes of key between elegant prose and obscenity. "Well," Fred said, "that's the way I want it and that's the way it's going to be."

The language bothered neither his twin sister nor his mother. Charlotte was able to ignore it and focus on the sensitivity of the book, which moved her deeply. Her only known objection to Fred's work came two decades later, when she said she didn't like *Last Notes from Home* because he called her "the old lady." When Fred pointed out that "I've always called you 'the old lady,' " she replied: "But now I *am* an old lady!"

It did concern Fred that people would read the book the wrong way and that they might take their feelings out on his mother and sister. Not long before *A Fan's Notes* reached the stores he went to Charlotte and Frances, to whom he said, "Now, I want to warn you, you're going to get obscene calls when the book comes out. There are going to be people who think that it's just a terrible book. These same people are out there reading *Portnoy's Complaint* and books like that. Whatever I wrote, there's not one thing in *A Fan's Notes* that's going to rouse some young child."

Goaded by Segal, Harper & Row took pains with the book. It was handsomely printed and bound, with an excellent dust wrapper. The cover, in subdued purple and red, featured an evocative drawing by James Spanfeller. Its most memorable feature, though, was on the back: a small, amateurish photograph of Fred, slightly out of focus. Clean-shaven, he looked upward toward the lens. His eyes were wide open and totally defenseless. He had the helpless, vulnerable look of a wounded animal. Because in later years he affected a Hemingwayesque style, complete with beard and projecting belly, people tended to forget what the author of *A Fan's Notes* looked like. That picture was him, the real Fred Exley.

As publication day neared—September 1968—Fred's mood was difficult to ascertain. He seemed to be feeling positive about himself, but did not seem to know how to handle the possibility that good fortune awaited him. He did not expect to make much money from the book, though he was ready to welcome any that might come his way, but he was apprehensive about the reception awaiting him in the literary world. He may have been a mad dreamer from the cold cow country, but he still wanted acceptance and respect. David Segal knew this and circled the wagons before the first shot was fired. He told the *Watertown Daily Times:*

Fred Exley is probably the best natural writer I have ever come across. By this I don't mean he doesn't work at it; just that what comes out has the immediacy and directness that readers mistakenly associate with ease of writing. Anybody who has ever tried knows that, in fact, this is a terribly hard effect to achieve. Exley also has an enormous talent for story-telling, by which I mean that he has a grasp of the proper length and shape natural to any given story and all his stories are both about themselves and about something else.

Besides which there is an almost searing honesty about this book, a tough-mindedness which sets it apart from other fictional memoirs that have been appearing in the last few years. I contracted to publish this book four years ago when it was unfinished and during those years my enthusiasm for *A Fan's Notes* has done nothing but grow. It is a marvelous book, and a talented book, and a commendable book, and I love it.

A Fan's Notes IS NOT FOR THE FASTIDIOUS. ITS LANGUAGE is occasionally rough and its structure is messy. Its virtues are energy, passion, humor, candor and a prose style that often achieves genuine eloquence as well as originality. Its weaknesses are its coarseness, its unimaginative anti-Americanism and its tendency toward excess. But there is no such thing as a novel—for it is as a novel, rather than as a memoir, that the book must be measured—without weaknesses. The strengths of *A Fan's Notes* are so formidable that they sweep objections aside. It is an amazing book that reveals more with each reading.

It opens with an eloquent if somewhat unconvincing disclaimer:

> Though the events in this book bear similarity to those of that long malaise, my life, many of the characters and happenings are creations solely of the imagination. In such cases, I of course disclaim any responsibility for their resem-

blance to real people or events, which would be coinciden-
tal. The character "Patience," for example, who is herein
depicted as my "wife," is a fictionalized character bearing
no similarity to anyone living or dead. In creating such
characters, I have drawn freely from the imagination and
adhered only loosely to the pattern of my past life. To this
extent, and for this reason, I ask to be judged as a writer of
fantasy.

Necessary though that paragraph may have been in order
to fend off libel suits, and supple though its prose most certainly is, in essence it is legalistic prattle. Though there are
characters and incidents in the book that are largely fictional, at heart it is a work of autobiography that was
slightly altered for, as has already been mentioned, legal
rather than editorial reasons. In a letter to Francena in
advance of publication, Fred said that "the law firm made
me change everything so it would be a novel, though one
woman editor at Harper remarked 'I don't know who this
Patience was, but whoever it was I'll bet she cries all
through the parts about herself.' " Those are not the words
of a man who had created "a fictionalized character bearing
no similarity to anyone living or dead."

As many writers of fiction would be quick to point out,
such considerations really do not matter; novels should be
judged on their merits rather than their autobiographical
elements. But because *A Fan's Notes* has struck such intimate
notes for so many readers, because its characters are so convincing and its passion so intense, because it stakes a large
claim on the reader's sense of reality, the question of what is
"real" and what is not has aroused intense interest.

Suffice it to say at the outset, then, that most of the people in *A Fan's Notes* are carbon copies of people in Fred's life. No attempt is made to disguise the members of his own family. "The counselor" is Gordie Phillips; "J." is Jack Scordo; "Mr. Blue" is an actual aluminum-siding salesman in Albany; "Patience" is Francena and "my twin sons" are Pamela. Apparently there is no single model for "Bunny Sue Allorgee," though Fred once told a newspaper reporter that at the time the book appeared the original Bunny Sue was living with her husband, a prosperous professional man, in a fancy house with their four children, a statement that rings more of fabrication than of fact; but some of the emotions Fred felt during his romance with her probably paralleled some of those he felt during his romance with Jeanne Adams. The only characters who seem to have sprung full-blown from his imagination are Patience's sister, "Prudence," and her husband, "Bumpy."

The narrator is a man named "Fred Exley," sometimes called "Ex," as his father was as well. Many years later, in *Last Notes from Home,* Fred claimed that "I have never written a single sentence about Frederick Exley except as he exists as a created character," but in the most obvious sense this is simply untrue; the Fred Exley we get in *A Fan's Notes* and everything else he wrote is the man himself, pure and unvarnished. But in another sense the claim is valid: the Fred Exley who speaks to us in this "fictional memoir" is the *real* Fred Exley, unencumbered by any desire or need to conform to the expectations of Watertown and social convention. It is here that his sensitivity is permitted to rise to the surface, that he allows himself to feel, think and say things the real Fred Exley could not. This is an important distinction, but it must not cloud the truth, which is that *A Fan's Notes* is an exercise in self-portraiture.

The book's structure is convincing and effective, but it is not neat. It moves in circular rather than linear fashion. As it opens Fred is assaulted, while he awaits the beginning of a Giants game on television, by what he imagines to be a heart attack but is actually the result of too much alcohol. He describes his life as a teacher of mediocre, indifferent students at a fictional town called Glacial Falls, and gives a vivid portrait of himself as football spectator at his favorite watering hole, the New Parrot. He also introduces one of his central themes, "that even in America *failure is a part of life*." He goes off to a motel with a boy who, like Fred himself, has suffered a loss in love but has started to recuperate from it by picking up an available girl; Fred listens to the rutting noises in the adjacent bed and gloomily reflects, "I hadn't come very far over the years—no farther really than from one 'gang bang' to another, save that I had learned . . . that tomorrow the pain would be even greater."

Following his hospitalization for his "attack," and a lecture from the nurse about his drinking, Fred introduces two of his most important characters. The first is Earl Exley. He recounts in the most moving terms a trip to New York with his father to meet Steve Owen, the famous coach of the Giants, to propose a game between the Giants and Watertown's Red and Black; the notion is of course preposterous, Owens says so with little effort at kindness, and the puny nature of his father's "fame" is made painfully evident to Fred. Immediately thereafter he describes his jealous admiration for Frank Gifford, his Southern California schoolmate and a figure of national, as opposed to merely local, consequence; it is here that he imagines himself shouting at

Gifford, "Listen, you son of a bitch, life isn't all a goddam football game!" and thereby makes a connection between Gifford and the central theme of failure's inevitability. This section ends with an amusing account of attending a Giants game in the company of a preternaturally preppy Wasp family, whose members are far more interested in putting themselves on display than in watching the game below.

After a somewhat artificial transition, Fred lands in Avalon Valley, where he meets the good-hearted Dr. K. and befriends a fellow patient named Paddy the Duke, who challenges him to find out what it is in him that drove him into that place. It is Paddy who awakens Fred to the idea of "sadness" and its connection to alcoholism, which in turn enables him to begin to face up to himself. This process is accelerated in the next section, the heart of the novel, in which young Fred Exley goes to Chicago, discovers the pleasures of urban life, and meets Bunny Sue Allorgee.

Her surname obviously is no accident. She is the allegorical embodiment of all that is most alluring and most awful about America. On the one hand she is beautiful beyond imagination, not to mention healthy and peppy and happy, "the girl I had sought to allay my grief at USC and been too leper-like to find, the girl I had sought all my nights in the Village, and the girl for whom I had waited way off there at the Broadmoor in Colorado Springs." Soon he takes her to bed—later he realizes that *she* had taken *him* to bed—where to his amazement and chagrin he is unable to perform. Then he meets her impossibly dreary parents behind their bland suburban façade, "and, oh lord, the thought that this might indeed be my heritage, my fate, struck me all the more impotent." He learns that "Miss America, it seems, was a Lolita after all and had been indulging herself, with a remarkable lack of discrimination, since a high school full-back had taken her at a scarcely pubescent fourteen." What the all-American girl offers is not fulfillment but humiliation and emasculation:

> . . . I came to understand that my sexual failure in the end redeemed me, saved me from an almost certain castration. The failure was never to recur, so that I have no way of understanding it save in the light of that place, Chicago, at that time, a time when more than any other I felt at one with my country, and with that American girl, Bunny Sue. Had I gone erect with the awesome passion that I then felt for everything, had my penis mingled with that honey-dripping, corn-bred womb, who knows that I ever could have walked away?

Thus rescued from American convention, Fred finds himself back at his mother's house, where he bedevils his stepfather and, during his "Journey on a Davenport," confronts further memories of his father. He winds up back at Avalon Valley, where he is visited by the girl in the Mercedes. Upon his release he makes his way to the counselor's apartment in Albany, where he meets Mr. Blue, "the perennial mock-epic hero of his country, the salesman, the boomer who believed that at the end of his American sojourn of demeaning doorbell-ringing, of faking and fawning, he would come to the Ultimate Sale, conquer, and soar."

The book's concluding two sections contain a rush of events: Fred's marriage to Patience; his failed attempts at writing; his encounters with his dour sister-in-law, Prudence, and her amiably goofy husband, Bumpy; the birth of his twin sons; the legendary tackle by the Philadelphia Eagles' Chuck Bednarik that puts Frank Gifford on the sidelines and gives Fred "a glimpse of my own mortality"; a trip to Florida during which he commits himself to his writing vocation; his return to Watertown and his writing room; the counselor's disbarment; Fred's resumption of teaching and his discovery, as he cradles his mother's dying dog, that he has the strength to go on living.

Of the novel's weaknesses, the least important is the occasional crudeness of its language. For one thing, what seemed at least mildly shocking in 1968 is commonplace three decades later. For another, Fred actually uses rough language rather selectively in *A Fan's Notes,* as opposed to his incessant and self-indulgent use of it in his two subsequent books, so that when it appears it acquires a certain force. The most important point, though, is that this coarseness stands in clear contrast to the sensitivity, bordering on delicacy, of the book's overall tone; whether intentional or not, in this regard it is a legitimate literary device.

What is actually more distracting than his language is Fred's unremitting mockery of his native country. The problem is not that his complaints are illegitimate but that most of them rarely are imaginative or interesting. "I loathed the America I knew," he says, and offers this as starting point for the book: "A long time ago in that private hospital I had learned that hate can redeem as well as love, but I was yet to articulate this truth and hence did not know that in writing a book hate is as valid a departure point as love." But the hatred he feels for America is not clearly or originally articulated. It turns out to consist of little more than diatribes about America's obsession with "physical comeliness," its "utter and unending lack of imagination," its insistence upon work, no matter how degrading. It is unfortunate that Fred refers in passing to *Lolita,* for in so doing he merely emphasizes how thin and puerile his own social criticism is by comparison with the subtlety, wit and inventiveness of Nabokov's.

Finally, there is the matter of Mr. Blue. Read apart from the rest of the book, this section is entertaining, well written and provocative. The problem is that it doesn't fit inside *A Fan's Notes.* When one friend complained about it, Fred responded that the section is "a picture of America," but if he really believed that, he was deluding himself. However amusing it may be, the section is too long and takes the focus away from Fred. This is more of a jolt than any of the abrupt shifts from polite to coarse language, for it leaves the reader wondering where the book is now going and to what purpose.

None of these shortcomings is trivial, but none is fatal. What is of far greater importance are the book's remarkable strengths. The first of these is its prose. So much of it has been quoted to this point that there cannot possibly be any need to quote further by way of illustration or proof. Though Ernest Hemingway was a powerful influence on certain aspects of Fred's writing and his notions of the literary life, his prose draws heavily upon his two literary heroes, Nabokov and Scott Fitzgerald, with perhaps a touch of Henry James thrown in for good measure. In the end it is his own prose and no one else's, but its delight in elaboration and circumlocution clearly reflects the benign influence of Nabokov, and its lush romanticism is of a piece with Fitzgerald's. When Fred quotes Fitzgerald—"I left my capacity for hoping on the little roads that led to Zelda's sanitarium"—he is paying tribute as well as making a point.

The skill with which he draws his characters is astonishing. His fellow natives of Watertown may have thought that writing about one's own life is easy, but no one who has attempted to do so can possibly agree. Making real people seem real is difficult because the writer must choose among the many aspects of them that he knows as opposed to merely inventing those that serve his convenience. Fred made the counselor so vivid and engaging that he became, in the minds of many readers, a larger-than-life folk hero, and his portrait of Wally Richardson is painted with so much feeling that it brings tears to the eyes. As to his portrait of Fred Exley, that is best of all. Nothing in writing is harder than making oneself interesting, appealing and important to other people. The small outburst of memoirs in the last decade of the century has inadvertently demonstrated that most writers are not half so interesting as they imagine themselves to be. But the Fred Exley of *A Fan's Notes* is one of the great characters of American literature, Huck Finn gone alcoholic and dissipated but still lighting out for the territory, putting as much distance as possible between himself and civilization. Raucous and obscene, demented and obsessed, wounded and vulnerable—there is within him something that touches and surprises every reader. Surprises, that is, because, as David Markson has pointed out, the reader who finds himself astonished at the messy life of this ne'er-do-well man suddenly is shocked into the awareness that this same ne'er-do-well man has written this unique and beautiful book, that he has a way of talking to the reader that is direct, intimate and irresistible.

The honesty of the book verges on the terrible. No one was ever harder on Fred Exley than Fred Exley himself. Each of his faults is isolated, explored, magnified. He does not let himself get away with anything. If in the end he achieves a kind of peace and self-justification, it is because he has earned it. Whereas many writers write about themselves for purely therapeutic reasons and neglect to draw the reader in, Fred knows at every step that honesty is the only way to convince the reader, and he offers it up in vast amounts. If reading the book is a thrilling experience—and it is—it is horrifying as well, for the spectacle of a fellow human being exposing his innermost self with such unflinching candor is not always easy to watch.

It should be mentioned, too, that Fred's use of football is unmatched in American literature. Only Bernard Malamud, in *The Natural,* comes as close as Fred does to exploring the metaphorical implications of sport in American life. One reason it is hard to believe Fred's reflexive criticism of other aspects of the United States is that his delight in the violence of this distinctly American game is so obvious and rich. No one has written more revealingly than he about how Americans live vicariously through the exploits of the "heroes" of sport, or about how capriciously "fame" can be awarded or withheld.

As this reminds us, Fred had the courage in *A Fan's Notes* to wrestle with large, important themes. The face in the American crowd has been the focus of many substantial works of fiction and nonfiction—Jack London's neglected novel *Martin Eden* (1909) is one of the first and best—but in few places does it receive such provocative consideration as it does in *A Fan's Notes;* the multilayered approach in which both Earl Exley and Frank Gifford are employed to consider the varieties of fame and its meaning, as well as the connections between the famous and the ordinary, is genuinely original. Few questions matter more to Americans

than the place of the individual in a populous, heteroge-
neous, unfeeling society; Fred's examination of the psychological weight of this is powerful and haunting. Similarly,
the novel's slant on that hoariest of our national obsessions,
the "American Dream," uses sexual and domestic material
in order to shed light on the price of success; Fred's criticism
of American society is not, as noted, unduly interesting, but
the dramatic situation he sets up is startling and apt.

A Fan's Notes has established a place for itself. Walk into
any self-respecting bookstore and you will find a copy of the
Vintage paperback in the fiction section. This edition sells
steadily if not spectacularly and is used from time to time in
college courses on twentieth-century American fiction.
Though we do well to view with skepticism the claims of
the academy to have final say on which books are voted up
and which voted down, this endorsement by people who
make their livelihood in the study of literature is not to be
taken lightly. It meant a lot to Fred whenever he heard that
he had made his way into another syllabus. But *A Fan's
Notes* is also read by "ordinary" readers, who are drawn to it
not for study but for pleasure, of which it offers much, and
for illumination, with which it is also generous. They are
likely to do so for many years to come, and *A Fan's Notes* is
sure to be cited alongside *Invisible Man* and *The Assistant*
and *The Adventures of Augie March* and *The Moviegoer,* to
name just four with which it deserves favorable comparison, as one of the literary monuments of its time and place.

As publication neared, Fred's "anxiety increased tenfold."
For part of the summer of 1968 he fled to a rented cottage on
Cape Cod, where he tried to get started on his second book

and where he played host to a reporter from the *Watertown Daily Times,* whose three-part series on the new author and his book put Fred on the local map once and for all. He thought often about Edmund Wilson, around whom that second book eventually would revolve, and waited "for the reviewers to notice me, in some odd way honestly believing that within the narrow orbit of which Wilson was the nucleus nothing really bad could come to me."

As it turned out, he had to wait quite a while. Perhaps because first novels often get lost in the deluge of big, commercial fall books, perhaps because a novel "about" professional football seemed of questionable seriousness, it was not until December that the first of his two most important reviews appeared. It was by a staff reviewer for *The New York Times,* Christopher Lehmann-Haupt, who liked to read and write about sports; he found it "a singularly moving, entertaining, *funny* book, certainly among the half-dozen best I've read this year," and perceptively analyzed both its strengths and weaknesses. The second appeared a month later in *Newsweek,* where Jack Kroll described the book as "a beautiful attempt to tell the truth" and made particular note of its "single tone of narrative accuracy whose authentic sweetness is the measure of its truth-telling."

Other reviews dribbled in from other places, but none meant as much as these two. The first gave him the imprimatur of America's most famous newspaper, the hometown paper of the publishing industry, and the second broadcast his name around the country. One reader whose eye was caught by *Newsweek*'s photo of Fred, leaning against a bar with a beer beside him, was his old friend of Chicago days, Jerry Raskin. They had been in touch only occasionally for years, and Raskin knew nothing about Fred's new life as a writer. He was bowled over. When he managed to reach Fred by phone, the first thing Fred said was, "You wouldn't believe it, wouldja?" Before the conversation ended he threw in the usual closer: "I may have to borrow some money from you."

In Watertown the book caused great excitement. More than two hundred people came to Robinson's Book Store for Fred's signing, at which he appeared in coat and tie, looking more like a proper establishmentarian such as James Gould Cozzens or John P. Marquand than a literary rebel. In almost no time Robinson's sold four hundred copies of the book, which pleased Fred but also gave him a misguided optimism about the commercial marketplace. "They are extremely optimistic in New York," he said, "and the early reviews have been favorable." He should have listened more closely to David Segal, who, over drinks with Fred before publication, said with a sardonic laugh, "That fucking book will sell about seven thousand copies if it's lucky, have a great word of mouth among your peers, but it'll win the Faulkner, it'll win the Rosenthal, and with an awful lot of luck it'll win the NBA. But the main thing is, Exley, once they're between covers books have lives of their own that neither you nor I nor anything whatever has any control over and *Notes* will be around and around and around." Segal was right; by late 1969 Fred had received only $2,800 in royalties, but different rewards awaited him.

Around publication date Fred came to New York, but Harper & Row's publicity department wasn't able to find much for him to do; newspapers weren't interested, and neither were television or radio broadcasters. The result was that he hung around the office, getting in the way. Finally a publicist came to the sales department and got Mel Zerman.

"You love authors, right?" she said. "Can you take one off my hands?"

"Who is it?"

"Fred Exley."

"*Fred Exley?!* The author of *A Fan's Notes?*"

"Yes. You like it?"

"I love it. It's a great book."

"Well, I can't get him on anything. He just sits around my office with nothing to do. I have work to do. Let me bring him in here."

So the woman brought Fred into Zerman's office. They started talking. The instant Zerman told Fred how much he liked the book, their friendship was sealed. It lasted the rest of Fred's life. Zerman, a short, trim man with impeccable literary taste, became one of Fred's most generous meal tickets. He was one of the many people who believed so passionately in Fred's talent that he was willing to put up with any misbehavior and extend any favor. When the two first met, Zerman was living in the suburbs with his wife and their children, and he usually saw Fred in Manhattan at lunch or at the Lion's Head. But after his wife's death in 1985 from cancer, he moved back to the city. Fred almost always stayed with him. He never hit Zerman for cash, but he drank everything in the apartment and came and went as he wished. He regularly wrote to Zerman, occasionally passing along a bit of news but almost always asking for free copies of a number of new books, ranging from novels to how-to books on interior design. Fred also made Zerman a member of the inner circle of his telephone network, calling him at all hours with publishing questions: Did Mel think Lynn Nesbit was doing a good job for him? Was Bob Loomis playing games? Was Random House being tight with him? Was Random House prepared to go higher? Zerman always tried to answer these questions, but as usual Fred wasn't listening, wasn't interested in answers. He listened only to himself.

"Writing is such a lonely business," Fred told a friend who had written to congratulate him, "you work so much in the dark, and you are always asking yourself if anybody is going to get your message. It goes without saying, then, how gratifying it is to know that you have moved one or two readers. . . ." In fact the book was steadily acquiring readers, and admirers. The most dramatic evidence occurred when it was among the five finalists for the National Book Award for Fiction, to be announced in New York on March 10, 1969. The other finalists were John Barth, Jerzy Kosinski, Joyce Carol Oates and Thomas Rogers. Fred "would have happily conceded the award" to any of these except Kosinski, whose *Steps* he found "by far the weakest entry, pretentious, brutal, repulsive if you will." Early in March he learned from Lynn Nesbit that Kosinski was the probable winner. He "decided against going to New York and playing the good loser."

There was better news elsewhere. *A Fan's Notes* won the William Faulkner Award for best first novel of 1968 and received a special citation, the Richard and Hilda Rosenthal Award, from the National Institute of Arts and Letters. The award is given to "that work which, though not a commercial success, is a considerable literary success." Fred had been notified of this somewhat dubious distinction by the chairman of the institute's grants committee, John Cheever, with whom he had already struck up a correspondence. In 1966, when Fred was still utterly unknown, he sent Cheever a fan note. As Cheever told his friend John D. Weaver: "A man named Exley wrote to say that he liked the stories. I thanked him briefly. He then called collect from Miami and asked me to post five hundred dollars bail. He had just smashed up a saloon and knew I would understand."

The Rosenthal Award was presented to Fred at the National Academy and Institute in May 1969. He invited his brother, Bill, to join him, and "it was much to my surprise when he accepted." They went to the institute together, Fred in "a newly purchased Paul Stuart summer suit of a rigidly cut and demure gray." This seemed appropriate for "my first peek at the literati, if not ill at ease, at their austerely proper best, with legs crossed formally at the knees, hands crossed primly at the groins." He found the affair stifling but amusing. He was permitted to take his prize but not to give an acceptance speech, which on the whole probably was fortunate.

Fred welcomed the Rosenthal Award because it "carried with it some badly needed dough." He got more good news in that department a month later from the Rockefeller Foundation, which gave him a $10,000 writing grant; it was his first experience of the fine art of grantsmanship, though one of the relatively few profitable ones. He wrote a note of thanks to Robert Penn Warren, whose *All the King's Men* was one of his most treasured books and who had spoken generously to him about *A Fan's Notes*. He thanked Warren for "whatever part you played" in the Rockefeller grant and added: "As one who slept with 'King's Men' under my pillow at college, I want you to know that your compliment to me at the Institute was, in its way, infinitely more satisfying than the Rosenthal Award."

Another rewarding by-product of Fred's modest new celebrity was that he struck up a friendship with Frank Gifford. Someone had passed the book along to the football player, who read it with admiration and responded with characteristic modesty to his own role in it. He knew, as he once told Fred by letter, that *A Fan's Notes* transcended anything he had done on the football field, and he was plainly grateful both for Fred's esteem and for his further public expression of it in 1983, in an article for *Gentleman's Quarterly* called "The Natural." He became a willing, generous source of football tickets for Fred, once managing to come up with no fewer than ten for a big game between the Giants and the New York Jets; Fred attended with his retinue of Alexandria Bay buddies. In 1988, when *Last Notes from Home* was published, Gifford paid Fred the quite magnanimous compliment of giving a publication party for him at his apartment in Manhattan. This event, which was attended by many of the local literary and journalistic glitterati, was one of the high spots of the fall social season. Even Fred was there.

Within a few months of the publication of *A Fan's Notes* Fred started to hear from his own fan club. His files at the University of Rochester are filled with letters from readers, mostly but not exclusively men, who had been touched to the quick. "This is the first fan letter I have ever written in my life. . . ." is a typical opening sentence, or, "If you will permit a graceless play on words, this is a fan's note." A group of college students in Buffalo wrote a blind letter to Harper & Row, declaring that they had become "particularly intrigued" by *A Fan's Notes*; they wanted to discuss it with Fred himself. "The project has assumed something like the proportions of a pilgrim's quest so eager are we to get to know him," their spokesman wrote.

Nothing came of this request, but it underscored the extent to which *A Fan's Notes* had rapidly assumed the guise of cult book and Fred that of cult author. He touched people in singular ways. At Fred's funeral David Hirshey told about how Fred accidentally knocked over the glassware at an adjoining table in a restaurant. The man into whose lap the drink had spilled rose and said, "My God, you're Fred Exley, aren't you? You wrote my favorite book, *A Fan's Notes*. You can spill a drink on me anytime." A quarter century after the book's publication, a reader in Florida came upon it for the first time. He became "an instant and devoted fan" and "created among my several writer friends a definite local Exley cult."

The choicest of all Exley cult stories occurred during the 1980s. Fred paid a visit to Bob Loomis at Sag Harbor on Long Island, where Loomis had a weekend house. He scouted the local bar scene—in any new town, this was always the first mission he undertook—and determined at once that a place called the American Hotel was the spa of choice. He found a seat at the bar and hunkered down. Loomis stayed the course for a couple of hours, but at midnight called it quits. He gave Fred his telephone number. "Look, Fred," he said, "I'm right down the street. Call me anytime, and I'll come get you. But I've got to go."

Dawn came and there was still no word from Fred. Loomis checked out his room, where he found Fred sprawled over the bed, his trousers half down, out cold; Loomis called him "the only person whose self-winding watch stopped, because he didn't *move*."

"Fred," he asked, "what happened?"

Fred shook himself half awake. "Bob, you won't believe it," he said. "I'm at the bar and the bartender says, after a while, 'What's your name?' and I say, 'I'm Fred.' He says,

'What's your last name?' I say, 'Exley,' and he stopped in his tracks and pointed at me and said, 'September 1968.' "

It was the publication date of *A Fan's Notes*. The bartender brought Fred home that night, and every other night for the rest of his stay in Sag Harbor.

One predictable consequence of the éclat *A Fan's Notes* enjoyed was that it was bought by the movies. Initially it was purchased by Warner Brothers, with filming allegedly to take place on location in Watertown. As is so often the case with film projects, this one never came to pass. At one point the figure of thirty thousand dollars was mentioned as Fred's potential earnings from this venture, but his incomplete financial records and tax returns yield no traces of this. The movie that eventually materialized was made by Coquihala Films Ltd., a Canadian subsidiary of Warner Brothers, and briefly released in Canada in the fall of 1972. Directed by Eric Till, starring Jerry Orbach as Fred, the film is a well-intentioned disaster. It completely misses the point of the novel, and captures none of the interior tension that is so essential to it. Orbach, though earnest, is badly miscast; indeed the only person in the film who makes anything noteworthy out of his role is Burgess Meredith, playing Mr. Blue. The irony that the novel's least successful section should be the film's one bright moment needs no elaboration.

The film was never commercially released in the United States. If it had been, it would have sunk without a trace. It was shown once at the Kennedy Center in Washington, in January 1979. Fred did not attend. Someone in the audience—the letter in Fred's file has no signature—told Fred: "The audience looked like a meeting of a Frederick Exley fan club. I saw the paperback *Fan's Notes* sticking out of several pockets. One guy entertained himself—the showing was delayed a half hour—by reading passages out loud. A lot of intense looking current and former English majors— the kind that look like they wished they had an envelope or something to write poetry on during the day."

This account may have amused Fred but probably did not please him. A decade after the publication of his first novel he was well aware of what an insurmountable obstacle it presented to him. Part of the problem was discouragement. "*A Fan's Notes* came out in September and got its first major review in December," he told a writer for the *Chicago Tribune*. "It was nominated for a National Book Award. It won the Faulkner and Rosenthal Awards. And by the time it caught on, it was back in the warehouse and nobody could buy it. I was so disappointed that I couldn't write for a year and a half." But it went deeper than that. Whether Fred knew that he had exhausted himself as a subject in that book is doubtful, because he continued to write about himself for the rest of his life. But he quite certainly knew, however little he may have cared to reflect upon it, that he had reached heights he would never again attain.

He was a one-book writer, limited by his inability to get outside himself and by his knowledge that he had done the best he was capable of doing. "Unless one is a writer," he said, "it is difficult to comprehend with what passionate depths one comes to loathe one's own creation. . . . For years I had not kept a single copy of that book within a country mile of me. Neither had I kept a single review nor letter in praise of it." The second part of that passage is probably untrue, but the first is far more than mere melodramatic hyperbole. Fred was a writer, barely forty years old, and his best book had been written. Small wonder that when he went to Florida in the early 1970s and rented an apartment on Singer Island, he took a paintbrush and wrote on the wall behind his sofa, in letters a foot and a half high, these words:

A FAN'S NOTES SUCKS.

THE 1970S WERE FOR FRED A TIME OF CREATIVE DISAP-pointment and calculated self-mythologizing. He published only one book, *Pages from a Cold Island,* for which he was rewarded with the most devastating review of his life, and a handful of magazine pieces. He moved around and about from Florida to Manhattan to Hawaii to Alexandria Bay, the resort town on the St. Lawrence to which his mother had relocated not long after Wally Richardson's death. His romantic attachments were fleeting and of little signifi-cance. The premature deaths of two men to whom he was close were heavy blows. He did readings and other campus appearances, usually in a state of inebriation.

At the end of the 1960s Fred made a Manhattan home away from home for himself in a saloon called the Lion's Head, on Sheridan Square in the West Village. In the sum-mer of 1969 he was newly separated from Nancy and in the first stages of the long legal wrangling between them, but his Rockefeller grant gave him cause for optimism. The only significant stipulation was that he had to appear from time to time on the campus of New York University "and nod knowingly for the creative writing students." Since the university was at Washington Square, he required only a bar within easy walking distance to be set for the duration. The Lion's Head, which had opened a few years earlier, turned out to be just what he was looking for: "The minute I stepped down the three steps leading into the Head's bar— Joe Flaherty has accurately compared its decor to a fighter's dressing room in Hoboken—I was stricken with familiarity and knew that I was home." A decade and a half before, during his brief period in Manhattan following his graduation from Southern Cal, Fred had done much of his drinking at a place around the corner called Louis' Tavern, his companions there including young actors named Steve McQueen and Paul Mazursky. Louis' was long gone, but the Lion's Head proved a more than adequate replacement.

The Lion's Head was an egalitarian, offbeat place. One man who served behind its bar called it "the only bar in the world with Irish lovers, Italian intellectuals and Jewish drunks." Its decor was shabby, and its distinctive feature a section of wall covered with the framed dust wrappers of books written by the bar's habitués. It was a journalist's hangout rather than a literary salon, so most of the books within those jackets have long been forgotten, but it had a pleasantly collegial atmosphere. Like many places that cater to writers, the Lion's Head acquired over the years a certain affectation; some who hung out there were real writers, others were mere hangers-on or poseurs. Fred called it "a bistro frequented by poets, novelists, reporters, agents, editors, and camp followers." He could have added actors, musicians and politicians. Inasmuch as Fred had rapidly acquired a following among journalists, it was the perfect place for him; he would hear nothing but praise, and he would always be the center of attention.

Fred arrived at the Lion's Head that summer of 1969 with his papers from the Rockefeller Foundation in hand. The promise they contained of regular remuneration for the coming year was sufficient to qualify him for a tab that he ran steadily through the summer and into the fall. Bar tabs were, in Fred's financial world, unlike anything else. Bills for rent or utilities and loans from his friends meant little to him, and supplications from the Internal Revenue Service didn't mean much either, but a bar tab was sacred and to be honored at all costs. During an impecunious stretch his tab might scale the heights, but whenever he received a check he used part or all of it against that indebtedness. This was the case at the Lion's Head and, later, at the bars in Alexandria Bay among which Fred wended his daily way.

Fred's first afternoon at the Lion's Head was spent in the company of David Markson, a novelist whose style was far more literary than Fred's but with whom he immediately established a strong friendship. Markson was talkative, outgoing, inquisitive, formidably erudite and sharp, but hadn't a scintilla of pretense or pomposity. He published one novel, *The Ballad of Dingus Magee,* that enjoyed a fair commercial success and was made into a movie; his other books were lavishly reviewed but, being more literary in character, found fewer readers. He and Fred never talked about intimate matters, but had much to say about books and writers and fellow habitués of the Lion's Head; their talk and laughter went on for hour after hour. In those days Markson matched Fred drink for drink. When his wife, Elaine, took their children to the country for the summer of 1969, Markson dug in for what became an epic season during which a sober moment was as rare as a cool breeze.

Almost at once, Fred became King of the Lion's Head. He had his tab, his place at the bar, and his legend. His monologues ran into the night. Few remembered anything he said, except that it was funny, though rarely witty, and outrageous, though only infrequently offensive. The conversational competition was tough, but Fred always held his own and usually led the pack. In New York as elsewhere, stories about Watertown and Alexandria Bay were the entree on his bill of fare; he managed to bring the old hometown to life for those who had never seen it and whose own lives bore little resemblance to those of his friends back there or his own. He saw his native patch of cold country not merely as his private reality but as a novel, and he transformed it into one for those for whom he performed at the bar.

On one occasion Fred introduced a whiff of Watertown's less attractive side into the Lion's Head. In the course of an argument with a bartender he suddenly said, "If you say or do that again I'll throw your skinny Goddamned Jew ass outside and kick the shit out of you." That caused shock and disappointment, but it was so atypical of Fred's usual bluster and insult that it was allowed to pass.

Fred finally left the Lion's Head in the fall of 1969. In the men's room someone wrote on the wall, EXLEY, COME BACK, PARANOIA IS NOW PERMITTED. It stayed there for years. Fred always went to the Lion's Head when he came to New York, though as his friends there died off or sobered up, its allure diminished. As was true of every other place where he hung his hat, sooner or later he took it off the rack and headed elsewhere, never with a backward glance.

✧

By 1970 his itinerary had a new stopping place. That year his mother purchased, for three thousand dollars, a tiny house on Walton Street in Alexandria Bay, a few blocks from the St. Lawrence River. She decided to move to Alexandria Bay because Fred's twin sister, Frances, was doing laboratory work at the hospital there and she wanted to be nearby. Not long thereafter Charlotte's sister, Frances, acquired a house on Crossman Street. Although the Exleys had spent their vacations on Lake Ontario when Fred was a boy, Alex Bay, or "the Bay" as it is universally known, exercised a powerful appeal on them and many others in the region. The town is at the heart of the Thousand Islands, an area of great natural beauty and singularity, as described when Fred was young by the Federal Writers Project guide to New York State:

> The Iroquois called the Thousand Islands region Mani-tonna (the garden of the great spirit), because it corre-sponded to the happy hunting grounds of their dreams. An early French explorer looked out upon the island-strewn upper reach of the St. Lawrence River and exclaimed, "Les milles iles!" And the Thousand Islands they have remained, though there are more than 1,500 of them. Some of them are no more than projecting rocks with room but for a single dwarfish tree; others are rounded tufts of forest rising gently from the water; still others are miles long, supporting entire villages. Historical events and freak natural forma-tions suggested such names as the Lost Channel, the Nee-dle's Eye, Fiddler's Elbow, and Devil's Oven.

In the middle of the river only a few hundred yards from the center of Alexandria Bay stands Boldt Castle, on Heart

Island, built beginning in 1899 by George Boldt, a hotel dishwasher who in time became owner of the Waldorf-Astoria Hotel in New York City, as a gift for his wife. It is a huge stone structure, turreted and crenellated, patterned after the castles on the Rhine that Boldt had seen as a poor Prussian boy. It was never finished and, after Boldt's widow's death, fell into neglect and disrepair. A small part of it is now restored and open to the public, and its astonishing yacht house unfailingly produces gasps from boaters passing by. As Fred once wrote:

> One can best gauge the grandeur or Teutonic ostentation of Boldt's vision by describing only his houseboat, *La Duchesse,* one of 18 vessels he kept in his boat house on Wellesley (named for Sir Arthur Wellesley, the Duke of Wellington who defeated Napoleon at Waterloo) Island. A building big enough to house a Regimental Combat Team, the boat house has slips 128 feet long. *La Duchesse* is 106 feet long, has a beam of 26 feet, a net tonnage of 243, a 4.3-feet displacement, an all-steel hull (it was originally all-mahogany), its two stories contain a dancing deck, ten bedrooms, five bathrooms, two open fireplaces, a dining room and a salon.

Boats are essential to Alex Bay and the Thousand Islands. Many of the islands are settled, often with only a single dwelling; boats are the only way to get to and from other islands and the mainland. There is one bridge, the Thousand Islands International Bridge, six miles long when one adds up the several segments that leap from island to island, connecting the United States to Canada. The bridge was dedicated in 1938 by Franklin Delano Roosevelt, but its first customer is said by local legend to have been Earl Exley, who "with wire cutters severed the cable which had been strung across the bridge's entrance to bar *hoi polloi,* climbed into the back seat of a convertible roadster, and had himself driven over the arcing, sky-rising span, while in imitation of F.D.R. he sat magnificently in the back seat, his jaw thrust grandly out, and, hand aflutter, bestowed his benedictions on the lovely and (one somehow imagines) startled islands."

Early in its history the St. Lawrence was under the sway of smugglers who transported merchandise across the Canadian border. Eventually this was brought to a halt, or at least whittled down to tolerable size, but a tradition of lawlessness remains. The isolation provided by the islands, heightened by that already imposed by the winter weather, has encouraged an independence of spirit that leads people to live by their own laws and ignore those imposed by governments, whether near or far. Many of the men with whom Fred hung out in Alex Bay were of such a character. He once sent David Hirshey of *Esquire* a clipping from the *Watertown Daily Times* about an international drug bust in the islands in which more than thirty suspects were arrested. "I thought you and your fellow editors would get a kick out of the enclosed," he said, "that is, if they had any doubts about my claims to the village's 'utter lawlessness.' All those circled in the piece are well-known to me, some are even drinking and golfing buddies. . . ." Though Fred often exaggerated his intimacy with the underside of life, in this instance he was telling the truth.

The Bay's river rats, as they are commonly called, are part of its year-round population. Their numbers, as well as those of the area's law-abiding permanent residents, are small; the population of Alex Bay barely exceeds a thousand. But the numbers grow, the narrow streets become jammed and the harbor rapidly clogs up when high summer arrives and the tourist season begins. Many of the islands are owned by wealthy outsiders who pump a lot of money into the local economy but exist at a distinct remove from the year-rounders. This produces all the predictable tensions and resentments, but by the time Fred became a fixture in Alex Bay the river rats found themselves yearning for the days when they had only rich yachtsmen to contend with. After World War II, as the national economy bulked up and the wealth spread, Alex Bay and the Islands turned into meccas for day-trippers. They flood the town's streets, jamming into its T-shirt and souvenir shops, crowding the decks of its tour boats. The natural beauty of the region remains essentially unsullied, but its human character has changed. Fred and his friends did not think it changed for the better.

If the 1970s were a time of difficulty for Fred, nothing hit him harder than two sudden, unexpected deaths that occurred early in the decade. The first, at the end of 1970, was that of David Segal. By mutual agreement he had recently left Harper & Row and found his way to Knopf, where in all likelihood he would have been more comfortable, since it was receptive to the literary avant-garde and less awestruck by publishing tradition. But he wasn't given time to settle in. The excesses of his life caught up with him. He died of a heart attack in December 1970 at the age of forty-two. His death was a terrible shock to everyone in publishing, his authors most particularly. William H. Gass spoke for all of them in a tribute published by *The New York Times Book Review*. Segal, he said, "had his own views about the nature of fiction. They weren't mine, but stories shaped and salted to suit some 'dogma' he kept like a pet were not a requirement." Gass continued:

> He was always fiercely loyal to the quality he found, and he was able to detect quality so often where others could not because he really was willing; because his soul was in no sense commercial; because his mind was always free of protective doctrines; because good work was not a threat to him; because he did not find it necessary to feel superior to it; and because he did not require of every work that it be made over in his image. He was a holy father, perhaps, but not a holy ghost. And against all opposition, he persevered. He was not intimidated by reputation, nor did he enjoy snubbing poor unknowns or slighting unheralded manuscripts. A combination of such traits is very unlikely.

"Segal's name keeps popping up all over the place," Fred told Mel Zerman a couple of years later. "How much I want to do right to his memory!" However odd a couple he and Segal may have been, Segal had given Fred a support such as every author dreams of from an editor. Never had Fred been more in need of that. *A Fan's Notes* had been the work of an unknown, but its successor would be the work of an author with a reputation to uphold and a cult to please. Fred, for whom affection and praise were mother's milk, needed both, especially as he was anything but confident about his work in progress.

That had not been the case at the outset. In the fall of 1969 Fred told David Markson, "Still sober, and the book goes well, frighteningly so as it appears to be coming much too facilely; perhaps it has something to do with 'Notes' taking me so long and now I can't accept that the new book, coming so rapidly, is as good as it appears to be." It wasn't. After writing several hundred pages, Fred jettisoned it. He began work on a loosely connected series of journalistic pieces, exploring his own life as usual but also interviewing Gloria Steinem and Edmund Wilson's daughter, and facing down Norman Mailer.

Fred had no publisher, though Harper had the customary option on his first book following *A Fan's Notes* and had even given him a $7,500 fellowship in lieu of an advance on a specific work in progress. With Segal gone, Fred's chief contact at Harper was Mel Zerman, whose position in sales put him outside the editorial mainstream but whose interest in and knowledge of serious literature gave him more leverage than sales personnel usually enjoy outside their own department. As early as 1970—after Segal's departure from Harper but before his death—Zerman had made the "radical suggestion" that Fred let him be his editor. His goal, he told Fred, was "not at all" to become an editor: "I simply want you to stay with us and I feel confident that by being an editor, and a good one, I can accomplish that end."

Nothing came of this. The situation had gotten complicated. Harper wanted to put Fred in the hands of an editor, a woman, whom Fred liked but of whose unqualified support he was not confident. There was reason for this, not so much because of her own feelings but because Harper itself was backing away from Fred. Lynn Nesbit was trying to get as much money as she could for Fred's second book, and Harper wasn't sure he was worth what she was asking. So the usual publishing minuet began in 1973, with sample chapters of *Pages from a Cold Island* going out to a half-dozen publishers. Harper was one of these, but the winner was Robert Loomis of Random House, who signed Fred up in 1974 with an advance of fifty thousand dollars.

He and Fred scarcely knew each other. They met at the Lion's Head before the deal was closed. It was a pleasant encounter, though Loomis found it peculiar that Fred never looked directly at his eyes while they talked but focused vaguely on his forehead. It wasn't until they knew each other better that Loomis came to understand that Fred rarely looked anyone in the eye. Later still, in *Pages from a Cold Island,* Fred explained himself: "My paranoia has never permitted me to be an eyeball-to-eyeball man; I view my eyes as an open window through which one too facilely discerns my transgressions; to the unavoidable discomfort of my colloquist my eyes evade and I shyly isolate a chin, a forehead, an ear...."

Loomis was Fred's age, a Midwesterner who had gone south to Duke University. After college he went to work for the publishing firm of Rinehart, which he left to join Random House in the mid-fifties. Eventually he was joined there by his old friend from Duke, William Styron, whose novel *Lie Down in Darkness* had been published by Bobbs-Merrill. Styron remained with Loomis and Random House thereafter. He was one of the living writers whom Fred most ardently admired, and Loomis was able to bring about a meeting of the two. It was a friendship that Fred cherished, all the more so since Styron always spoke with self-effacing generosity about Fred and *A Fan's Notes.*

Fred's connection to Loomis, which lasted the rest of Fred's life, was of immeasurable importance to him. "Without Loomis's support and confidence in me," he said, "I'd probably be dead." He thought that the dust-wrapper copy

Loomis wrote for *Last Notes from Home* perfectly explained the book: "Has a writer ever had a better editor than Bob Loomis? He said it all there. He told everyone how to read me." So far as Fred was concerned, Loomis was "*really, really* a gentleman, an altogether uncommon phenomenon in The Fucking New America."

The two men became firm and loyal friends, though Fred never violated his tacit strictures against intimate conversation. Superficially they seemed irreconcilably dissimilar. Fred was drunk, sloppy, disorganized, unproductive, while Loomis was orderly, patient, self-disciplined. But Loomis's mild manner and trim mustache were misleading. He had a quick wit, enjoyed a glass of Jack Daniel's bourbon whiskey, could talk at heroic length. Fred visited Loomis and his wife, Hilary Mills, on a number of occasions; he came to regard them with clear and deep affection.

Both Bob and Fred often remarked on the curious irony that Bob had been the editor of *Steps,* the book that beat out *A Fan's Notes* for the National Book Award. One could scarcely imagine two writers, or two men, less alike than Frederick Exley and Jerzy Kosinski. But one of Loomis's greatest strengths as an editor was that, like David Segal, he accepted his writers for what they were and did not try to shape them into something else. He gave Fred careful guidance on both of his last books, but he did not try to impose his own views or tastes; on his visits to Sag Harbor, Fred could often be found at the dining-room table, sober, plugging away at revisions Bob had suggested.

What is sad is that by the time he came to Bob Loomis, Fred was a burnt-out case, as a writer if not as a man. It was the fate of this sympathetic and generous editor to preside over two books that, had their author not been Fred Exley, would probably never have been published. He tried to help make them as good as they could be, and left it at that.

The second death occurred little more than a year after Segal's. In the fall of 1972 Fred's brother, Bill, retired from the army. He was stuck at the rank of colonel and was disenchanted with the war in Vietnam. He was no dove, but he felt that the whole country of South Vietnam wasn't worth a single American life, and the slaughter of innocent Vietnamese at My Lai by trigger-happy American troops troubled him deeply. He had been a gung-ho interventionist when the American involvement began, but that had changed. Now he just wanted to get out, to retire to his house in Hawaii.

What he did not know was that he was terminally ill. At the rigorous physical examination customarily given retiring military officers, doctors discovered that cancer had launched a full-scale invasion of his body. The case was hopeless: "After the quacks kept calling him back for further X rays, they finally cut on him last November, took a peek, closed him back up, stitched him, and put him on the new cancer-controlling drugs. That's when the telephone wires between my hometown, Alexandria Bay . . . , and Honolulu began crackling."

Bill and Fred talked. "Under no circumstances did [Bill] want the old lady, considering her health and her inordinate trepidation of flying, to come to Hawaii. He was being readmitted to the Tripler Army Hospital, he looked ghastly, man, ghastly, 'like a piece of shit,' and in no way did he want the old lady to see him in that condition." But Charlotte was adamant. She and Fred flew west. She was "an aging and ailing mother, a woman twice widowed, a woman who nightly peruses her Bible and accepts literally the three score and ten years meted man by that book, a woman not uncognizant of having buried two spouses and now en route to lay to rest her eldest progeny, a woman doubtless mightily distressed at the unfairness of [Bill's] being taken at forty-six and perhaps even chagrined and perplexed that her Bible had seemed to betray her."

They got to Hawaii in February, just in time for "the three days of Bill's dying." Charlotte stayed with Judy Exley while Fred holed up with an old Watertown friend Jo Cole and his wife, Phyllis. It was the first of many times that he was to take advantage of their hospitality, first in Honolulu and then on Lanai, to which they soon moved. Seeing Bill, whom Fred in *Last Notes from Home* calls "the Brigadier," was terrible. He was thirsty and asked for a cold, noncarbonated orange drink:

> The Brigadier's cancer had become so pervasive that both his liver and kidneys had failed; indeed, they had placed a sheeted cage discreetly over his stomach to protect our virginal eyes from the severe distention of his abdomen, and it was apparent that any additional fluids would force the doctor the inconvenience of employing a catheter to draw off the excess urine. When we protested his request, the Brigadier's smile was utterly devoid of bitterness, rue, regret, sorrow. Then the Brigadier threw his arms out from his sides in the most good-natured gesture of futility, as though to say, "C'mon, guys, is it going to make any fucking difference?"

The next afternoon Bill died. He was buried with full military ceremonies, including a seven-man honor guard the members of which, "from their vacant-eyed mute rigidity," struck Fred as having spent "one too many days in the line in Nam." This probably had more to do with conspiracy theories about Vietnam and the CIA and My Lai and Bill that Fred was nourishing in his imagination than with the truth. But there can be no doubt that Fred was deeply upset. He wore a disheveled raincoat; standing slumped by the grave, he looked forlorn, haunted by Bill's death—he had now lost his father, his stepfather and his brother—and by his own mortality, which on that warm Pacific day pressed insistently upon him.

His health was actually rather good, considering that he mainlined alcohol, smoked heavily, ate irregularly and often poorly, and took no exercise beyond the walking that he did on the rare occasions when he was sober. Not long before Bill's death he'd had one small scare—he canceled a visit to New York in December 1972, wiring Markson, DOCTOR JUST NIXED MY TRIP LIVER NEEDS REST SEE YOU IN SPRING— but he was healthy enough to go to Hawaii and then, upon his return, to set himself up in Florida once again.

As usual when in Florida, Fred sponged when free room and board were available, but he established himself more or less steadily on Singer Island, which had been described in a legal document involving one of Fred's friends as a "shabby resort area, the hub of Palm Beach County's drug culture, and a hothouse of whoredom, practiced both formally and informally." This suited Fred fine. He was more likely to observe local illegalities from the sidelines than to participate in them, but the raffish seaside atmosphere appealed to him:

From left to right facing the sea, Beach Court housed the editorial and business offices of *Alfred Hitchcock Mystery Magazine;* the Island Beauty Salon; a Quick Stop grocerette (open 7 a.m. to 11 p.m.); Schneider's Orange Tree and Beer Barrel (hamburgers served on one side of the Western-type swinging doors, beer and wine on the other); the Surf Apartments (cheap); and the Seaview Hotel, from where I wrote and where beneath me in the Islander Room the nightly floor show featured a comic named Mother Tom and two dancers (variously named Rosa Bella, Harlowe Angel, Sunny Day, Burning Embers, Miss Charlies, Hallow Ween, Honey Hush, Pandora's Box, et al., they came and went) who removed their gowns to the taped music of *Aquarius,* permitting lonely salesmen and rowdy cowhands in from Pahokee and the Glades to see the G-strings jammed up their raunchy bums.

Singer Island was Fred's base of operations, but he was often out of town. The college lecture circuit had discovered him, and from time to time he climbed aboard. Once he reported to a friend that "for no apparent reason I'm suddenly getting many offers to read at prices I've never been offered before." He turned most of these down; but over the years he showed up at Northwestern University, Eureka College, Humboldt College, Jefferson Community College and other places. His fees were not immense—the largest recorded is $1,650—but the money was welcome and the adulation even more so.

So far as Fred was concerned the high spot of his academic itinerary was the University of Iowa. He first went there in April 1972, for a reading and a party at the Writers Workshop, whose staff treated him royally. The event went well, so Fred was invited to come back as a guest lecturer in the fall. The head of the fiction program was John Leggett; the other permanent staff member was Vance Bourjaily. Besides Fred, the workshop had as guest lecturers that semester Gail Godwin and John Irving, both still relatively unknown but much admired by Fred, Godwin in particular, whose *The Perfectionists* he found "beautifully written" and whose later novel *A Mother and Two Daughters* he considered "one of the very great novels written in America in the last two decades." Thanks to Fred—or so he claimed— the workshop also had lectures in the fall of 1972 by William Styron and John Cheever. The latter had once told Fred that it might be just as well if they never met, given their shared fondness for strong drink, but when he arrived three days before his reading, drinking was foremost on his mind. "No sooner were we on the highway than John reached into his raincoat pocket, pulled out a plastic flask containing gin," and "took a healthy swig." He kept swigging through his entire stay, abetted by Fred, who "prior to John's arrival [had] left in his room two quarts of scotch and two of gin." Each morning they met "for the Irish-affliction ritual, shaky cups of coffee, then in a tacitly mannered way made our way chuggingly up the hill and began our morning round of campus saloons."

Fred was in heaven. He was in the company of a writer whom he worshiped in a place that worshiped writers. As he and Cheever strolled through Iowa City, merchants opened their doors and greeted them effusively. Cheever was astonished, and assumed that the hullabaloo had been caused by Fred, who in just a couple of months had become widely known in town. What they actually wanted was to be introduced to Cheever: "Certainly there can be no other city in the very heart of Babbitt Country where a purveyor of plumbing supplies would leave his business establishment in the hope of shaking Cheever's hand."

Predictably, Fred got involved with a student, a young woman half his age: "Our relationship was very incestuous and the only pride I take in our mutual seduction of one another, for with that age difference, unless one is a lecherous roue, the girl has to take the initiative, is that she wasn't one of my students and therefore had nothing to gain by way of a grade." This affair lasted past Fred's departure from Iowa at semester's end, but had fizzled out by the mid-seventies, when he discovered that the woman had found a man of her own age. He feigned dismay but can only have been relieved, for romantic commitments—or any others involving emotion, sacrifice and responsibility—no longer held any appeal for him. Twice burned, forever shy.

Fred loved Iowa and longed to go back. In the early 1980s, a period of severe financial need, he quite desperately tried to get another appointment there. He believed himself the victim of what later became known as the white-male syndrome. The workshop was "getting all kinds of shit from some group called Affirmative Action for not hiring enough chicks, spades, spics, even Eskimos!" As "an English-Irish-Episcopalian, I had to check every single box NO," which may or may not have had anything to do with his failure to get the job. As a consolation prize he was invited to give three readings during the fall semester, but the fee was far less than he had hoped to receive.

At Iowa and elsewhere during this period Fred was hard at work on his literary persona. It is impossible to say how much of this process was calculated and how much of it unconscious, but there can be no question that it was a major project. As has been mentioned, he had incurred no stylistic debt to Ernest Hemingway—quite to the contrary—but he found the Hemingway persona appealing. He liked the image of Hemingway hard at work in his Parisian garret, "locked up in a room getting on with the business of his life," while lesser people frittered away their time in sidewalk cafés. He was fascinated by the unlikely friendship of Hemingway and Joyce, "this big brusque laconic midwestern Hemingway with his contemptible high school diploma out of Oak Park, Illinois, mucking about with this petite half-blind vitriolic Irish genius educated to Latin and Greek by the Jesuits." He believed that Hemingway and Joyce "were bound together by being on the same arduous, near-reverent pilgrimage . . . of what the French call 'breaking the language,' of doing nothing less than taking English and making it their own," and that though he "shouldn't . . . presume to mention my name in the same sentence with Joyce or Hemingway," this was what he too was doing. He didn't copy Hemingway's style, but he "always accepted Hemingway's—he was not in the least a learned man despite his protestations—dictum that if a scene is drawn faithfully and truly enough the symbols and the myths would necessarily evolve." Beyond all that, he had a certain admiration for the manner of Hemingway's death, by a shot to the head, fired by his own hand. He found this honorable and courageous.

Hemingway was the last figure of the romantic era of American fiction, the era that he embodied along with Scott Fitzgerald and Thomas Wolfe. By the same token Fred's was the last generation of writers to fall heavily under his influence, to believe that hard drink, hard living and, if it be so ordained, early death were the appropriate ways of living the literary life. So Fred turned himself into Hemingway in miniature. He permitted himself to develop a lordly belly that he carried with pride and he grew a beard of Hemingwayesque thickness. He had his photograph taken by a gifted photographer named Mark Jury, who caught him bent over a cigarette, holding a match to it. He looked so much like Papa, one could scarcely tell the difference. Not merely did he use this photograph on the covers of many hardcover and paperback editions of his books, but for a time during the 1970s he reproduced it at the top of his private stationery: no name, no address, just Papa Exley.

Many of his friends noticed that in the absence of serious writing he was devoting much time and energy during this period to the shaping and perfection of Frederick Exley,

Mark Jury

Author. Few of them found anything attractive about the process. He was not overbearing in the Hemingway manner, but not merely did he strive to look certifiably authorial, he began to talk and write about himself in exalted terms. "I know that many of my peers—from [William] Gaddis to Styron—think I might be putting down the most significant American trilogy of my time," he told David Hirshey, and continued:

> I'll tell you a story, which you are free to accept or reject as you see fit. Last summer I was visited by a half-dozen undergraduates from McGill U. in Montreal. They told me that the favorite American Lit. lecturer there devotes an entire lecture to the Steinem section in *Pages,* calling it something like "the best sustained piece of humorous writing in the English language." McGill is the Harvard of Canada.

Fred wanted literary respect and fame, yet he recoiled at much in literary culture. Though he liked to correspond with writers—Cheever, Styron, Gaddis, Don DeLillo, Richard Ford, Kurt Vonnegut, James Dickey—he was uncomfortable in the places where they hung out. The ceremony at the American Academy and Institute in 1969 had made him uneasy, and so did Elaine's, the highly mannered Upper East Side hangout of literati who imagine themselves several rungs higher than the scriveners who gather at the Lion's Head. "Shit, you've got all kinds of hacks hanging around the bar of Elaine's trying to get a table next to Gay Talese," he said, as though there were any difference between that and trying to cozy up to Joe Flaherty at the

Lion's Head. He felt a deep ambivalence about New York City itself. Coming to Manhattan as a published author was important to him, especially if the trip involved a subsidized stay at an expensive hotel where clerks and waiters fawned over him. He was dazzled by Manhattan and wanted to dazzle it in return. Among his New York friends he spoke often about Watertown, almost always comparing it disparagingly with the big city. Yet he was spooked by the "stony refusal to esteem me" that he had sensed there during the 1950s, and always felt insecure, defensive, wary. He was always glad to go there, and he was always glad to leave.

Fred hated bookish back-scratching, "this tit-for-tat horseshit that goes on in the literary racket," though he was not above engaging in it for his own benefit or for that of fellow writers whose work he respected. He was uncommonly generous with blurbs. "The only reason I give quotes to young writers," he told David Markson, "is that *nobody, but nobody,* gave *A Fan's Notes* one. However, I'm being driven from my small apartment with bound galleys and am going to have to put a stop to it with my silence." One editor was so persistent about getting these meaningless encomia from Fred that finally Fred just let the editor write the blurbs himself, then blithely vetted them.

Fred was caught in the trap of fame, or what passes for fame within a literary culture that is itself a pitifully small part of the larger American culture. As has been true of many others, he wanted fame on his own terms. He was too proud to go begging for applause and adulation. He expected this to come to him. It was, after all, part of his birthright, his entitlement. When it did not come in the measure he expected, he turned bitter and vindictive. There were times when he worried about it more than he worried about his work, and he permitted it to distract him from the business at hand. Given that his supply of raw material had been exhausted this is perhaps no great loss, but the spectacle of this gifted man fretting over the inconsequential and ephemeral is not pretty.

"Something truly marvelous is happening," Fred told Mel Zerman in July 1972. "As you've probably guessed by now, I've had grave reservations about my new book, something more profound than 'second-book jitters,' and I have miraculously found a way to work this Wilson stuff in and give the book the substance it was screaming for."

Edmund Wilson had first presented himself to Fred as a subject of more than purely literary interest during the "Journey on a Davenport" described in *A Fan's Notes*. "Coming inadvertently across an autobiographical sketch of his, I was at first astonished, then pleased, to learn that but a few miles south of me, at Talcottville, the legendary critic inhabited for part of the year a limestone farmhouse of his own, an heirloom from his mother's side of the family. This was a remote and flimsy parallel upon which to build a literary romance, but I had little to cling to in those days. . . ."

It was also a remote and flimsy conceit around which to construct his second book, but more than three years into the writing of *Pages from a Cold Island,* Fred was rapidly approaching desperation. The manuscript wasn't holding together. It needed a focus; Fred decided that Wilson could give it one. As in *A Fan's Notes,* he constructed the book around a distant figure whose success he could contrast with his own failures; he meant the book to be "about a writer as failure" as well as "an elegy to Edmund Wilson." He worried about it right to the end, his confidence shaky: "Because I made so many changes in galleys, [Random House] wouldn't even send the page proofs for fear I'd start fucking around with it and cost them another small fortune in printing costs. Too, I wanted to add another epigraph—a quote from a letter from Joyce to Ibsen—but feared that the reader might think it was terribly pretentious and that I was setting myself up as fucking Joyce!" The epigraph was added.

The finished book works to some degree as an account of "a writer as failure," but not at all as "an elegy to Edmund Wilson." The familiar book-within-a-book device—*Pages from a Cold Island* is, among other things, about its author's failure to complete a book called *Pages from a Cold Island*—is employed with modest cleverness, but in the process Edmund Wilson gets lost. Though there is one extended passage about an encounter between Fred and Wilson's typist, and another about his meeting with Wilson's daughter, the Wilson material for the most part is halfhearted and perfunctory. Fred is far less concerned with literary matters in this book than with defining and enhancing the Exley mythology.

Pages from a Cold Island is separated from *A Fan's Notes* by seven years in time and light-years in character. It contains obligatory gestures toward confession and self-mockery, but its tone is boastful. Its characterization of Fred's sexual organ as "the frightful hog" sets the tone for everything else. The book's language is too often gratuitously crude, its treatment of women quite genuinely offensive and its self-infatuation off-putting. In his first book Fred had presented himself as a true misfit, a man constitutionally incapable of living in the ordinary world in an ordinary way, but in his second he comes forward thumbing his nose, strutting across the page, waving "the frightful hog" for all to admire and envy.

Part of the problem the book presents is that in an understandable effort to cash in on the small celebrity he had acquired, Fred was trying to sell off pieces of the work in progress as they rolled through his typewriter. To a degree he was successful. *Playboy* paid $4,600 for the Gloria Steinem section, and *The Atlantic* bought some of the Wilson material, for another $1,500. Fred needed the money. But the effect on the book was to heighten its patchwork quality; the connection between Steinem and Wilson, or Mailer and Wilson, never becomes sufficiently clear and never leads to any thematic business of weight or consequence.

Pages from a Cold Island, which was published in April 1975, opens with Wilson's death. It moves quickly to Singer Island, where its pace briefly picks up as Fred writes with flair about that scruffy place in which he took such wry pleasure. For no real reason there is a sudden digression in which Fred fantasizes about the man who wrote the off-the-wall right-wing editorials that the New York *Daily News* specialized in at the time. It is a brief but funny passage that, since the book is no longer in print, deserves to be quoted in full:

> ...I had an overwhelming urge to seek out the editorial writer and buy him a few drinks. So unrelentingly nasty

was his tone that for years I'd been certain he didn't believe a word he wrote—nobody bright enough to construct a grammatical sentence could believe it—and that he knew his loonily Olympian derision was doing more for peace than any march on the Pentagon. I had even fantasized a romantic image of him. Certainly nobody in the *Daily News* offices ever saw him. He was an inch over five feet, crabbed, wasted, and he chain-smoked nonfilter cigarettes that left nauseous stains on his fingers. Winter and summer he wore an Army-issue wool khaki greatcoat whose hem brushed his shoe tops, and on awakening each noon he gathered up his ball-points, his yellow lined tablet, his *Thesaurus* and the morning newspapers and went to the Lion's Head on Christopher Street, took a spartan wooden table in the back room and ordered black coffee and two ounces of top-shelf brandy, Hennessey or Martel. After a half-hour of diligently perusing the newspapers, with the aid of his *Thesaurus* he wrote his editorials in fifteen minutes, sent them by messenger to the *Daily News,* and passed the rest of the day pacing himself on imported St. Pauli Girl beer and writing unpublishable poetry about the childhood he'd imagined he'd had in Crosby, S.D., remembering always the afternoon he'd had a single beer with Dylan Thomas in the White Horse Tavern.

The next section is a rather sentimental account of running into a Floridian in a bar, a man who talks proudly about the house he owns in a panhandle town; Fred subsequently learns that the little town—and, presumably, the man's house—has been destroyed in a storm. Then, at great length, Fred recounts his preparations for his interview with Steinem. His "overriding desire was to discover who she was apart from her cause," but no such discovery is made. Though the meeting of the feminist princess and the macho skeptic has its amusing aspects and a few droll Exleyisms—"when she offered her hand, said hello and smiled and I had a glimpse of those big even white teeth I was visited by angels who whispered to me that something quite like heaven would be to put my tongue in Gloria's mouth and just loll around on her back fillings before even moving up those marvelous ivory monuments up front"—the cumulative effect is no greater than that achieved by newspaper or magazine journalism.

At last Fred returns to Wilson. He introduces himself to Wilson's secretary/typist/confidante, takes her on a picnic, but comes away from the encounter with nothing revealing. The same goes for his meeting with Rosalind Wilson, the writer's prickly daughter; it produces some decent writing, but nothing else.

The book ends in a rush. Fred attends the Academy and Institute ceremony at which he is presented the Rosenthal Award, a chapter from which selections have already been quoted. He makes fun of Shirley MacLaine and other limousine-leftist celebrities riding the George McGovern presidential bandwagon. He runs into Norman Mailer and labors at insulting him, which is not hard to do. He ends up in Iowa, in the embrace of a girl—"Miss Middle America to a heartbreaking fault"—who seems meant to provoke memories of Bunny Sue Allorgee.

Fred watched assiduously for the reviews; as is true of many writers, he was never to be believed when he said that he paid no attention to them, that they didn't matter. He was in Hawaii, protesting too much: "There is no escaping, even over here . . . on the out island of Lanai. My paranoia dictated that I come over here to 'hide,' avoid reading the reviews, sober up, and get my head into some kind of shape should the worst happen to the new book." In the next paragraph he gloated over an advance copy of *Playboy*'s "almost embarrassingly generous" notice: "That they should all be so kind!" In May he told Mel Zerman that he "did not understand" Jack Kroll in *Newsweek*, that Paul Gray in *Time* had been "rather patronizing," but that he had "seen some rather embarrassingly great stuff from around the country, Larry McMurtry in the Washington Post and Geoffrey Wolff's front-page of the L.A. Sunday Times." He'd heard from Loomis that there would be a piece in *The New Republic* mentioning "what an asshole Kazin is."

The review of *Pages from a Cold Island* by Alfred Kazin appeared in *The New York Times Book Review*. It stuck in Fred's craw then and for the rest of his life. The most influential literary supplement in the United States had published a damning review of his book by the critic who was, in the minds of some, the linear successor to Edmund Wilson himself. Though Kazin handed Fred a bouquet—he called *A Fan's Notes* "a good, amazingly personal book" and Fred "a talented writer"—the review moved in a direction that hit Fred where he hurt. "Through a film of famous characters, scenes, narrative techniques, [Exley] no longer knows his life from the book he has made of it," Kazin wrote. Fred lived solely in order to write about what he lived. Kazin's closing paragraph was a slap in the face:

> It is all a riot, of sorts, full of the special bravado—*I am not afraid to say anything about anybody:* that is Exley's flourish. No one will get mad. Much as I enjoy reading Exley, I am

depressed by how instantly perishable it all seems. It's too much of an act—the act it had to be in order to get itself written. So it's not a novel either, but a magazine-smart piece of writing by a very good writer who is afraid of letting us see the dilemma that made this book necessary.

"He doesn't know," Fred wrote in the margin of the review—meaning, presumably, that Kazin was making a statement about Fred's literary motives that he could not substantiate. Perhaps so. But all the evidence Kazin needed is in the book itself. It is strained and contrived. The contrast with *A Fan's Notes* is glaring. In his first book Fred seemed to be writing almost against his will, forcing painful confessions out of himself in the hope of finding meaning in them and pleasure for the reader. In *Pages from a Cold Island* no such urgency is to be found. The only necessity is to get the book written, to fulfill the contract, to amplify the persona and its legend. As Kazin properly—and, it might be added, generously—pointed out, there is some good writing in the book. Fred always wrote well, except when a fit of grandiosity seized him. But good writing doesn't amount to much unless it says something, and in *Pages from a Cold Island* Fred had nothing to say. Those who rushed to Fred's defense or publicly castigated Kazin—*mea culpa*—were wrong. Kazin was right.

Not merely that, but his review was far more devastating to Fred than its actual contents warranted. Kazin was amused by much in the book and did not hesitate to say so. Fred's anger may have been aroused by the headline over the review—"A bad book by a good writer, Frederick Exley"—which Kazin did not write and which rather misrepresented what he said. No author likes to be told that he has written a "bad book," especially in a headline that may be all many people will ever read about the book.

Fred was on the phone for hours grousing about Kazin, about the *Times Book Review,* about fate. His conversations were more one-sided than ever, as he tried to talk away the hurt he felt. He thought the review was unfair—it wasn't— and he wanted his friends to come to his defense. The man who had just finished dishing it out to Gloria Steinem and Norman Mailer and Shirley MacLaine couldn't take it himself.

PAGES FROM A COLD ISLAND DID NOTHING FOR FRED'S REPU-
tation, but it did have one positive effect. The magazine
excerpts he sold to *The Atlantic* and *Playboy* opened a new
source of income and readership for him. For the remainder
of his life, writing for periodicals—*Rolling Stone, Esquire,
Gentleman's Quarterly, Inside Sports*—kept Fred one step
outside the poorhouse. It also gave him a way to test-run
sections of his third and last book as he struggled to give it
coherence and meaning.

In his journalism as in everything else Fred was self-
preoccupied and high-handed. He wrote well when he
chose to, but no matter what his subject he always ended up
writing about himself, with the result that several assignments never got into print. He assumed that magazines
existed to cater to his fancy, so he wasted a lot of his time—
not to mention his editors'—cataloguing his demands and
pleading for funds to subsidize them.

The most important of his journalistic associations was the least likely. In the fall of 1976 Fred visited San Francisco, en route home from a prolonged stay with the Coles in Hawaii. As he was wont to do, he quickly made connections with the city's journalistic community, one of the most notable members of which was Jann Wenner, the founder of *Rolling Stone*. That magazine of rock music and countercultural politics was still based in San Francisco, where it had been started in 1967, though its move to New York was in the offing. Most of its young readers were drawn to *Rolling Stone* by its features and gossip about rock musicians, as well as its reviews of new recordings, but it had done some thorough reporting—especially during the rock festival in Altamont, California, where a spectator was killed by Hell's Angels hired to guard the Rolling Stones—and it had attracted attention in mainstream journalism for the adventuresome prose of Hunter Thompson and other "gonzo" writers. Its influence was beginning to be felt in conventional newspapers as well as at *Harper's, New York* magazine and other places hospitable to the "new" journalism, a central premise of which was that the reporter was as interesting and important as the story, if not more so.

Fred had absolutely no interest in the world *Rolling Stone* covered—he once told Wenner that "I'm neither into fucking music nor into fucking movies"—but his self-absorption made him a prime recruit for the new journalism and his need for money was acute. He was thousands of dollars short of earning out his advance for *Pages from a Cold Island,* and money for the last volume of the trilogy had not started coming in. There is no evidence that he had thought about a career in journalism in any systematic way, but he liked journalists, he had done that brief stint on the *Palm Beach Post* and he was receptive to any ideas that involved money.

At a party he was introduced to Wenner. Paul Scanlon, the managing editor of *Rolling Stone,* was also there. Scanlon was closer in age to Fred than to Wenner, and was an ardent admirer of *A Fan's Notes.* Wenner asked him, "Would you like to meet Fred Exley?" Scanlon replied, "Are you kidding?" Fred struck him at first as incredibly drunk, but he talked in a circular, hypnotic manner that Scanlon found irresistible. For two hours they talked, in the course of which Fred told Scanlon that he was well into a third book; Scanlon got the idea into his head that *Rolling Stone* should serialize it.

Fred represented the book as an account of his brother's military service and an exposé of the various clandestine activities in which he fantasized that Bill had participated. From the beginning there was confusion at *Rolling Stone* about what sort of book it was to be. Scanlon understood that it was a work of fiction, while Fred left Wenner with the impression that it was to be reportage of a sort, albeit a novel. Wenner thought Fred was going to penetrate the CIA and solve the mystery of his brother's career. The prospect excited him. The espionage establishment was high on the hate list of his young readers; exposing it would attract wide attention and enhance the magazine's journalistic standing. By the same token, having Fred's byline in the magazine would be a strong sign that *Rolling Stone* was serious about writing as well as about popular music.

In the late winter of 1977 Fred showed what he described as one third of the book to Scanlon. "Perplexing business, this," Scanlon reported to Wenner. "In overall theory it's a wonderful idea," but carving out publishable excerpts would be a challenge. He wanted to do it, but his assessment was realistic. "Running the first excerpt would constitute a certain commitment to the readers and to Exley," he said.

"Are you willing to make it? Can it be reasonably done, given our ongoing and worsening space problems?" Furthermore: "Being a patron of the arts is one thing, and I think it would be a coup for RS to run a reasonable number of excerpts. I also think Exley is running the old shell game on you, which is the time-honored prerogative of the artist. *Ars gratia artis*. Where would it all end?"

Wenner decided to take the gamble. He and Lynn Nesbit negotiated a deal giving *Rolling Stone* exclusive North American rights to as many as six excerpts from Fred's work in progress. For this *Rolling Stone* agreed to pay twenty thousand dollars in three installments, over and above any expenses it covered for him. The agreement was confirmed in May 1977. Amazingly, the first installment appeared one month later, presented by the magazine's editors with "enormous pride." A second installment appeared in October 1978, the third in February 1979.

At the outset Fred was a pleasure to deal with. The magazine did fritter away a few hundred dollars on a trip to Hawaii, where Fred attended a reunion of some of Bill's military friends; he was drunk throughout, made some unintelligible tape recordings and came away with nothing more than the unfounded suspicions he'd had to begin with. His hopes of unearthing startling disclosures were further disappointed when a prominent investigative reporter dismissed them out of hand in a peremptory letter.

So there was not to be an exposé, but Fred did turn over three entirely publishable pieces: an account of his journey to Hawaii, containing numerous digressions; the story of James Seamus Finbarr O'Twoomey, a fellow passenger on that flight; and a portrait of Robin Glenn, the latest of Fred's fantasy women. All of the excerpts were delivered on time and in pristine condition, typed neatly on bond. The only problem was that they tended to run long. Scanlon got Wenner's permission to go to Alexandria Bay and do the cutting with Fred's help. Fred was living in a small apartment; Scanlon stayed at the Edgewood resort nearby. For three days they played golf, went fishing, took a boat tour of the St. Lawrence. Each morning they met at the Dockside, one of Fred's favorite bars, where he jolted himself into action with vodka; at night they moved from bar to bar, with *Rolling Stone* picking up the tab at each stop. Finally, on the fourth day, they awoke ferociously hungover and, when they met at the Dockside, guiltily agreed that the purpose of the visit had not been accomplished. They sat down in Fred's apartment and cut the O'Twoomey section in an hour and a half. Fred insisted on driving Scanlon to the airport in Syracuse, a hundred miles to the south. He drove in the lifelong drunk's manner: very, very slowly.

The excerpts ended in February 1979, but Fred's relationship with *Rolling Stone* continued for several more years. He wrote several pieces, only one of which made it into the magazine. That one was about drugs and professional football, which he delivered in the spring of 1983; the magazine carried it in September. The next year he went to London, where he interviewed Sarah Miles, the actress, with the intention of writing a profile of her for *Esquire*; for *Rolling Stone* he interviewed Michael Herr, the author of a nonfiction book about Vietnam, *Dispatches,* that had caused a considerable stir among the New York intelligentsia. He also attempted a profile of Mary Margaret Humes, a young woman from Watertown, a former Miss Thousand Islands who hoped for a career in Hollywood.

All these articles suffered from the same shortcoming: they were as much about Fred as about their ostensible subjects, if not more. Wenner rejected the Michael Herr piece, sending a kill fee of $1,000, because it "is not susceptible to a rewrite." An editor at *Gentleman's Quarterly* to whom the article was later shown was more blunt: "Sorry, but I think you missed by the proverbial mile. The Exley persona just overwhelms this piece."

The National Football League piece cost *Rolling Stone* $2,438.87 in expenses, plus Fred's fee of $2,500, which was paid when Fred turned the piece in. He then proposed that the magazine underwrite a trip to New York City. He wanted five nights at the Blackstone, paid for via the magazine's American Express account, but was willing to compromise: "If Jann wants to get me a hotel I wouldn't be ashamed to bring a girl in, follow the same procedure with that hotel." He wanted round-trip airfare between Syracuse and La Guardia, $500 in expense money and some arrangement for transporting himself from Alexandria Bay to Syracuse and back:

> I keep forgetting to tell Jann my killer expense is getting from here to Syracuse, 100 miles away, and in a cab usually runs $75 plus tip. Without a credit card one can no longer rent a car, and without being on a payroll and realizing a steady income I don't have a chance of getting one, notwithstanding that in my palmier days I have, on credit, purchased cars, furniture, etc, etc. from the same bank, Marine Midland. I wrote the retiring chairman of Marine Midland, who was a schoolboy chum of my late brother Bill and he told me that under our present idiotic societal structure I did fall into a grotesque category but he would see what he could do before he went to sit in the sun, or wherever

retired bankers go. Damnation, I expect. Still, I don't hold out any hope that he'll help me.

Wenner was amused but unmoved. "I would be happy to handle the reservations for you out of this office, but I don't understand the rationale of why I am paying for it. The NFL piece is done. What's up?" Fred responded in high dudgeon: "I quote, from memory, from your own letter of a year or so ago, 'When we get the next excerpt I'll be happy to underwrite a few days in the big city for you.' " To which Wenner responded with a dry "I'm afraid we have substantially different interpretations of what 'underwriting a few days in the Big Apple' means." He agreed to "spring for two nights at the Blackstone Hotel, but that's it."

That was it, and it was also the beginning of the end of Fred's connection with *Rolling Stone*. He wanted fees and expenses but never got around to writing the articles expected of him, or wrote articles the magazine had no interest in publishing. He thought of *Rolling Stone* with affection—"You know something, Jann," he said, "you're the guy who picked me up off the streets of S.F. and gave me the encouragement to go on"—but he had nothing further to offer it, and it had lost interest in him.

It was therefore doubly fortunate that just as things petered out at *Rolling Stone* new opportunities arose for Fred at *Esquire*. In 1984 David Hirshey, the young New York *Daily News* editor to whom Fred had been so generous several years before, was hired by *Esquire*. He called Fred right away. "Guess what, Fred," he said, "you now have a home." Home being the place where they have to take you in, Fred shipped his *Rolling Stone* rejects over to *Esquire*. They met the same fate there. Over the years *Esquire* published only four pieces by Fred: a portrait–cum–personal reminiscence about Alexandria Bay, a discursive report on the 1987 Super Bowl that was mainly a report on Fred, a profile of sorts of the television personality Diane Sawyer and a posthumous extract from an unfinished novel.

Unlike *Rolling Stone, Esquire* had problems with Fred's pieces as they came in. There was nothing pristine about his manuscripts. It is not out of the question that Fred did not take *Esquire* as seriously as he did *Rolling Stone,* but this is unlikely given its long history of publishing major writers—albeit not usually their best work—including many whom he greatly admired. The probable explanation is that wrenching a piece of journalism out of himself was even harder than squeezing out an extract from a book, for he was inherently uninterested in it; as a result, once he finally got around to it, he did it hastily. The idea of an Exley piece was appealing to *Esquire*'s editors, but when reality checked in, it was ragged and required major surgery.

One time Hirshey went up to Alex Bay to beard the lion in his den. Like Paul Scanlon, he got the usual tour and met all the usual local characters. Hirshey was there to prod Fred about the Alex Bay piece. It took a year to get it out of him in publishable condition, and, as it was, the final version rarely transcended the ordinary. *Esquire*'s devotion to Fred was commendable, but it didn't get much in return.

Fred didn't spare Hirshey any of the griping and groaning that he inflicted upon Wenner. His correspondence is filled with complaints about other editors or contributors to the magazine and pleas for money. The most inventive of the last was filed after his trip to London in the fall of 1984;

it involved expenses incurred on the piece about Sarah Miles that was never published. He expected reimbursement for, among other things, "one Aran Isle sweater mentioned in piece," sixty-eight pounds; "dinner at Julie's also mentioned," forty pounds, "with tip, it was actually more but I can't recall"; and a child, "that little spoiled prick, hit me up for five pounds, which I gave him to get rid of him and of course I'll never see again—I don't of course mention this in the piece!" He'd bought traveler's checks at $1.21 to the pound: "So I figure $170.61. Is that right? It doesn't sound like enough?"

Apart from writing a piece about Watertown football in 1981 for *Inside Sports,* which *Newsweek* had established that year as competition for *Sports Illustrated,* Fred's career as a freelance writer produced nothing of consequence. By the late 1980s Paul Scanlon had moved to *Gentleman's Quarterly,* which had shortened its nameplate to *GQ.* He bought Fred's reminiscence about the Lion's Head. He was also the prime force behind the magazine's decision to establish a fiction award in Fred's name as a memorial to him. It is too early to tell whether any of the recipients will prove to be writers of lasting merit, but Fred would have liked the honor—no doubt he would have chalked it up to entitlement—and he would have delighted in the annual awards ceremony, held at the Lion's Head until its demise in 1996.

What is made clear by these rare ventures into magazine work—fewer than a dozen full-length published pieces—is that freelance journalism simply was not a career for which Fred was made, demanding as it does self-discipline and energy. He expected the magazines to come to him hat in hand, just as he kept expecting fame to arrive, and when they did not he got huffy and took a hike.

This was no great loss to periodical journalism, but it deprived Fred of a source of income at a time when it was sorely needed. By the time the 1980s arrived he was in genuine financial trouble. His debts rose steadily, he took no regular or irregular jobs, and his income from books was paltry when stretched out over all those years. Random House advanced him fifty thousand dollars for *Last Notes from Home*, in three installments, which was generous in light of Fred's previous sales history but provided scant support over a decade that was otherwise unremunerative.

There had been a disturbing premonition of things to come in the late 1970s, when Fred sold his literary and personal papers. This was accomplished thanks to the interest and diligence of Peter Dzwonkoski, who had left the Yale University library and had taken over the Department of Rare Books, Manuscripts and Archives of the Rush Rhees Library of the University of Rochester. Dzwonkoski was an admirer of *A Fan's Notes,* and he felt it would be appropriate that its author's papers be on deposit at one of the more prominent scholarly libraries in the part of the world about which its author wrote so eloquently. So he wrote to Fred, and after a brief exchange of correspondence paid him a visit.

Fred was living in an apartment on Bethune Street in Alex Bay. Like other visitors, Dzwonkoski was immediately struck by the tidiness of it. They chatted, went over the items in and on Fred's desk. Fred was polite, responsive and apparently sober. He excused himself while Dzwonkoski examined the material, then reappeared an hour later. He was drunk as a skunk.

For several months the negotiations were in abeyance. Dzwonkoski talked to a number of people at the university and queried rare-book dealers about the value of Fred's manuscripts and papers. The responses he received were not encouraging; no one thought they were worth much. When he told Fred this, the immediate response was, "You don't like my writing, you think I'm a bum." The truth was that Dzwonkoski was having trouble finding the money; often, feeling out prospective donors, he had to tell them who Frederick Exley was. Explaining all of this to Fred in a diplomatic way, he got an angry response that said, in so many words, bring all your scholars up to Alexandria Bay and we'll have a barbecue with my papers.

Patiently, Dzwonkoski told Fred that the market value of his papers had nothing to do with the real worth of his writing. He pointed out that for a long time after Scott Fitzgerald's death there was no interest in him or his work and his papers were worth nothing, but that subsequently his reputation rose and, with it, the price he commanded. Unwittingly, Dzwonkoski had struck the right note, for Fred's admiration of Fitzgerald was intense. He became cooperative. A buyer was found, a man named Robert C. Stevens who agreed to purchase "all extant manuscript material related to [Fred's] novels, all extant correspondence received by him and carbon copies of letters written by him, all photographs, portraits, newspapers and magazine clippings, and printed material containing material relating to Frederick Exley, and all books inscribed to him by other writers."

The price for this came to $3,500, a pittance. Dzwonkoski knew it wasn't much and knew as well that Fred's situation was dire. He arranged to purchase Fred's personal library for an additional $1,500; the money was paid but the books were never delivered. The agreement between Fred and Stevens was signed on December 7, 1978; four years later the papers were officially turned over to the university.

If the deal was demeaning evidence of the desperation into which Fred was sinking, it had two salutary effects: it put Fred's papers in a place offering considerably more security than any of his own residences ever did, and it encouraged him to save material in the future such as in the past he might have thrown away. He kept a box under his desk and tossed any old thing into it, from personal correspondence to boilerplate pleas from editors for blurbs. Most of what he saved is useless, but a significant amount of unique material is now in the Rush Rhees Library's files; it makes far easier the task of piecing together Fred's days and nights, at least for the last decade and a half of his life.

The 1980s started on another gloomy financial note. In March 1981 Fred received a $1,500 check from the American Academy and Institute "to assist you in your present financial emergency"; it was sent with the hope that "your health is improving and that this check will help to alleviate your more pressing problems." Two years later more alms arrived, a $500 check from the Writers Fund Committee of the New York branch of PEN, the international writers' organization; it came from a fund established to provide grants for "writers, residents of New York State, who find themselves in financial difficulties while finishing a book under contract or a play about to be produced."

There was only one bright spot. On Christmas Eve 1983, William Styron told Fred, "If you don't get a Guggenheim, it will be through no fault of mine. I laid it on so thick (saying such things as: In 25 years of making recommendations there is no candidate so highly regarded in my eyes, etc.)

that they will either buy it or reject it out of hand as preposterous, perhaps indecent." Another generous recommendation was provided by William Gaddis. In March 1984 the Guggenheim Foundation came through with a $21,000 grant, for one year beginning in April 1984.

"I'm $20,000 in debt, can't breathe for creditors," Fred wrote in 1983. This may have been a slight exaggeration, but it cannot have been much of one. In 1984 he itemized his debts for the benefit of his tax preparer; they came to a total of $11,000, all of it owed to friends in Alexandria Bay and New York City. His tax returns for the 1980s—the only period in which he saved them—are unremittingly gloomy. In 1980 he had gross adjusted income of minus $32; in 1981, minus $5,380; in 1982, minus $2,930; in 1983, $2,300; in 1984, $4,950; in 1985, $1,320; in 1986, $664; in 1987, $1,203; in 1988, minus $157; in 1989, $2,690.

These miserable figures did not dissuade the Internal Revenue Service from nipping at his heels. He requested and was granted an automatic four-month filing extension for his 1984 return, then asked that it be extended to December 31, 1985. In a memo to his accountant Fred wrote: "His blood pressure is occasionally so elevated, he has trouble focusing and when this form was returned he saw only the stamp of approval. The day after Christmas, when, with a friend's help, he started to make out his returns, his friend detected that the Internal Revenue Service had crossed out the Dec. 31 date and given him until October 15, 1985, as a final filing date." By 1987 the IRS was asking him about unpaid and unfiled taxes. It sent a representative to his apartment in Alexandria Bay, apparently in search of undisclosed wealth. After the agent had thoroughly reconnoitered the place, he declared that Fred owed the IRS

$3.09. Fred had no checkbook, so he got a money order in that amount from the post office and sent it to the IRS, after scrawling across the front, "Shove this up your ass." A couple of months later it was returned, uncashed.

Jack Scordo, acting as Fred's attorney, told the IRS that Fred "acknowledges that he owes money to the Internal Revenue Service for back taxes" and "is anxious to pay off the line." It turned out that he owed $565.90 for 1984. Somehow he paid it all off, but his loathing for the IRS was sealed for life: "What a bunch of Nazi cocksuckers, their behavior in an alleged democracy is unforgivable, and were not our congressmen such a bunch of limp-dicked, wishy-washy, timorous band of nothings, terrified of themselves being audited, they would long ago have destroyed that Fascistic Empire."

By 1985 Fred's situation was so dire that he thought the unthinkable: he considered submitting himself for regular and gainful employment. He wrote to John Johnson, Jr., managing editor of the *Watertown Daily Times* and son of its editor. Fred proposed to write a regular column for the paper: "I thought of one column a month to run, say, the first Thursday (or whatever day you prefer) of every month. At first I thought I'd ask for $1.00 a word, not to exceed $1500 a column should a piece run to 2,000 words or better. . . . Then I thought it would simplify greatly matters to ask for $18,000 a year for 12 columns, out of which I'd expect you to take the standard IRS, Social Security and hospital . . . deductions." Having thus stated the royal desires, Fred lapsed into self-pity: "Listen, John, my lifestyle dictates that I won't make it to 62, but I was 56 March 28 and brought to short thinking about these things. If you and your father would care to help me I'd do the best I could for you."

Johnson was understanding and sympathetic, but a newspaper is not an almshouse. Not merely was Fred's price ludicrously high—for $18,000 a year the newspaper could hire an ambitious young reporter and squeeze oceans of ink out of him—but there was no guarantee either that Fred would actually turn in his work on time or that it would be of interest to anyone except Fred. The offer was politely rejected.

All in all, by the mid-1980s Fred was in terrible shape. He had no money and no real prospects of any, and his flamboyant habits were beginning to catch up with him. An unsigned memorandum written during the middle of the decade tells a depressing story:

> Frederick E. Exley . . . is suffering from severe coronary artery disease—what internists call "uncontrollable angina." He is heavily medicated. Besides carrying the regular nitro tablets (Nitrostat 0.4 mg) he also wears Transderm-Nitro 10 patches (10 mg) on his chest, with a daily change. For blood pressure he takes 160 mg. of Corgard daily, for fluid both Diural and Aquatensen and for potassium Slow K (600 mg. daily). He is also suffering from incipient cirrhosis of the liver. Whereas the normal blood-test liver reading is 65, Mr. Exley's most recent test showed his at an alarming 192.

Fred's road to this depleted state was long and predictable. His first critical illness did not occur until the late 1980s, but there were plenty of warning signs. In 1972 his doctor called off Fred's trip to New York City because he didn't like what the liver tests showed. In the mid-seventies Fred told David Markson, "Two weeks ago I got dizzy and fell down. Had to be taken to the hospital where my blood pressure was diagnosed off the charts, was told I was lucky

I didn't have a stroke or heart attack which I was in the process of having. Stayed there and went through a battery of tests and everything was wrong, high blood sugar verging on diabetes, etc, etc, all related to booze of course. Am off the booze, was told I could never drink again, etc, and am on all kinds of medications. It catches up with one, does it not? If you tell the guys at the Head anything, you might tell them that! You yourself want to be around to enjoy your great success, don't you?"

It was easier for Fred to give sound advice than it was for him to take it. He was in this respect hopelessly weak, but it is the choice he made and nothing is to be gained by berating him about it. The temptation to be judgmental about him is at times acute, but he lived according to his own designs and apparently he chose to die by them as well. That there was an element of deliberate self-destructiveness in his refusal to quit drinking despite his doctors' urgings is entirely plausible. One of the reasons he regarded Ernest Hemingway's suicide as courageous may have been that it was a courage he did not share. He had his own kind of fortitude, as exemplified by his determination to keep on writing long after he had exhausted his subject matter and himself, but it did not extend to taking his life by force. Most of the people who knew him regarded him as a coward when physical confrontation arose; he would run from a mouse and, his claims to the contrary notwithstanding, he fled from a fight. Taking his own life by gunshot or any other violent means would have been wholly out of character. Booze accomplished the same end more slowly, which just gave him more time to drink.

THE YEARS OF FRED'S LONG, SLOW DECLINE WERE SPENT primarily in Alexandria Bay, with ever less frequent forays to Lanai, the Lion's Head and Florida. He made two trips to London, the first a pleasure and the second a near calamity, but otherwise he was content to hole up in whatever happened to be his Alex Bay address of the moment. He watched out for his interests carefully and, with one notable exception, rarely paid any rent.

At first, in the early 1970s, he lived with his mother at the little house on Walton Street, on a lot scarcely bigger than the house itself. They were completely comfortable with each other. The house was L-shaped, with a covered porch inside the L and a claustrophobic second story whose rooms had slanted ceilings. It sat on an unprepossessing side street lined with other clapboard houses and small businesses.

This first Walton Street period lasted until the mid-seventies, when the money came in for *Pages from a Cold Island*, making Fred moderately prosperous for the only time in his life. He moved into his own quarters, a first-floor apartment on Bethune Street that was owned by Frank and Connie Cavallario, old friends who owned Cavallario's steak and seafood house, the roof of which Fred could see from his apartment; they served hearty Italian food, which Fred loved on those days when he was eating, and they ran a busy bar where Fred's tab was open-ended and often ran well into the hundreds of dollars.

There was no tab at the apartment, for which Fred paid the Cavallarios about $150 a month. It was in a handsome old house that had been broken up into five apartments; the rear yard had a small swimming pool with a view of part of the harbor. Fred's unit had high ceilings and old molding. He decided to do it up properly, which is why he asked Mel Zerman to send him that book about interior decoration:

> Could you get me the book I've put the X on, Betty Pepis' *Interior Decoration from A to Z*[?] . . . I'll tell you why. As soon as I get my advance, I'm getting an unfurnished apartment here in town. Frankie Cavallario is giving me one cheap (it's over the restaurant overlooking the water!) and, depending on the size of my advance, I want to fix it up as nicely as possible, even if I do so by stages, that is as I have the money and go along. It occurs to me, too, that Harper has probably published this kind of book and would you ask your girl to check and send me whatever you have, though there's no sense in sending me specialized books like LAMPS or MAKING FRENCH PROVINCIAL WORK! You know what I mean?

Zerman knew exactly what he meant. He sent the Pepis book and one from the Harper backlist. "Both the old girl and I liked looking at the pictures" in the latter, Fred reported, "though most of the layouts are way too snazzy for Upstate." He'd assumed that the Pepis book "would tell about paints, how to do shelves, the best buys on lamps, and that kind of things—and all it was was more snazzy pictures that indicate nothing of cost, etc. etc." This led to an editorial recommendation: "... it seems to me that if you could find a literate decorator you would have a great and continuing market for a book that would tell a young housewife and clowns like Exley precisely how to go after a room, how to cut corners financially, I mean, *really*, a book which would assume that everyone is as dumb about the subject as I am." In fact a series of precisely such books was then in the works, under the authorship of the British decorator Terence Conran; whether Fred ever got his hands on them is not known.

The picture of Fred thus busily engaged in the domestic arts is not without its hilarious aspects, but it is also a reminder that there were limits to his disengagement from convention. The Bethune Street apartment was the only dwelling place he ever had that could fairly be called his own, unless one counts the places he briefly shared with Francena and Nancy. He didn't own it, but he paid his rent more or less on time and his legal address was there. He was proud of this emblem of success, loved its location in the heart of the Bay, and wanted to entertain his friends there. This he did with the same unlikely flair for social convention that he brought to the decoration of the apartment, though the actual design and furnishing were done by Fran, with two thousand dollars that Fred gave her for that purpose.

Bob Loomis visited Fred several times in Alex Bay and saw him in most of his different residences there, but the treatment he received on Bethune Street was far and away the most memorable. The apartment was tastefully furnished and impeccably clean. Loomis stayed at the Edgewood—its owner, Bud Hebert, was one of Fred's best friends in Alex Bay, and did him many favors both there and at his winter place in Florida—but spent his days and nights with Fred, either in the apartment or on the bar circuit. Fred gave a party in his honor. There was plenty to drink, but the party wasn't raucous and no one got sloppy-drunk, not even Fred. Gordie Phillips and many of Fred's friends from the Bay were there. A photograph taken at the party shows Phillips and his wife, Fred and Bob and their dates, and a fourth woman; it could have been taken at any prosperous household on any of the islands.

The Bethune Street period lasted until the late seventies, eating up a good part of the advances for the last two books. As the money began to wither away, economies became necessary. Fred could have tried to sponge off the Cavallarios, but that doesn't seem to have entered his mind. Instead he moved back in with his mother during the late 1970s. His next stop was a room upstairs over a bar called the Dockside in the heart of Alexandria Bay. If he was writing, he sobered up at his mother's, then went to the privacy of the Dockside room to write; if he wasn't, he could be found downstairs. The bar was owned by Mike Bresnahan, the son of one of Fred's oldest friends. As was always true of Fred's life in Alex Bay, he loved the raffishness of the bar, yet deplored its "world of witless macho shorthand, split in equal parts of four-letter words, sex, fish and sports tales."

Living over a bar was perfect heaven for Fred. He was on hand when it opened at eight in the morning, ready for his vodka pick-me-up, and often closed the bar down at two or three in the morning. There was no phone in his room, so if a call came for him at the bar, Bresnahan tapped on the pipe that ran upstairs, and Fred came down to answer it. Once the caller identified himself as Frank Gifford; Bresnahan thought it was a prank. Fred had a great affection for the Dockside, and made use of his upstairs room until the early 1980s, when a new friend and a new benefactor entered his life.

His name was Clark Reidel. He and Fred had first met in the early seventies. Reidel was manager of Rankin Motor Freight's trucking terminal on Wellesley Island and was romantically unattached. At the time he was living at the Edgewood; it was Bud Hebert who introduced him to Fred. They ran into each other at various local bars, especially Cavallario's. In 1976 Reidel left the area for a couple of years, but kept a mobile home there. Upon his return he and Fred saw each other more frequently, and their friendship grew closer. Reidel's mobile home became a refuge for Fred, a place where he could escape the tourist crush in the Bay, where he could read or watch videotapes or just sit and drink.

Like many of Fred's friendships, this one was unlikely. Fred's egalitarianism was no act. He didn't care what people did, whether they read his books or anyone else's—one of his best friends in the Bay claimed he had never read anything Fred had written—or what they looked like or whether they were socially respectable. If he liked them, he liked them. In Clark Reidel he found a soft-spoken man with a quiet sense of humor, a genuine admiration for Fred's work, and a willingness to listen for as long as Fred cared to talk.

By the mid-eighties Reidel's situation had brightened. He had bought a waterside lot on Wellesley Island, where he was building a house, and he had gotten married. Bobbi brought her children from a previous marriage to their union, and Clark brought Fred. They built a detached garage with an upstairs apartment and set Fred up there; they joked that they built the apartment to get Fred off their couch. He paid them no rent, but took care of all his expenses, which his immense telephone bills sometimes inflated to impressive proportions. A month's worth of phone calls could run Fred nine hundred dollars or more. He told Reidel: "I don't spend dough on clothes, fancy cars and other material things, Clarko. I do like to have a drink now and then, cherish my friendships, and I love to occasionally talk on the phone with my pals."

The Reidels' generosity to Fred was remarkable. It pleased them to play host to one of the area's few nationally known residents—about the only competition was Abbie Hoffman, the erstwhile counterculture leader, who lived near Alex Bay under the alias of Barry Freed in the late 1970s—but it pleased them even more simply to play host to Fred. He was as much a part of their family as any of Bobbi's children. He came in and out of their house without knocking or announcing himself; he raided their refrigerator and pantry. Sometimes he went into town to replace what he'd mooched, invariably returning in a state of outrage: "Do you know what they're getting for a box of cookies in the Bay these days?"

At times the Reidels imagined themselves patrons of the arts in the truest sense of the term, but they subsidized Fred without resentment. Fred had cast the same spell over them that he had cast over so many others. They put up with him when he was drunk, they nursed him through hallucinations, they watched football games with him. In return he gave them his friendship and an ample supply of Fred stories.

Once, early in their friendship, during the trailer period, Clark went out of town for a while. He returned to find mouse droppings in the trailer. He put out a few traps, and warned Fred about them.

"Why'd you do that?" Fred asked.

"There were some mouse droppings on the counter," Clark replied. "Maybe you didn't see them."

"Oh, thank God."

"What do you mean, 'thank God'?"

"I know where the mouse is," Fred said. "I've seen him every night. I'll be sitting there watching TV, and he comes right out of your bedroom, comes down the hallway, gets about two feet in front of the chair, stands on his hind legs and looks right at me. Then he walks right by me into the kitchen. Why, he's been here for about three or four weeks."

"Well, why didn't you ever say anything about it?"

"Because I didn't know whether I was hallucinating or not."

Clark's business often kept him on the road. One night Bobbi was alone in the house with the children. At the time theirs was the only house in their neighborhood. A report was broadcast that two or three convicts had escaped from a nearby prison. They were said to be armed and dangerous.

Bobbi found a shotgun, loaded it and prepared to defend her family. The night was dark and silent. She heard a noise, and a door scraped open. She was in the bathroom, poised, her finger on the trigger. She was just about to fire when something gave her pause. The noise was Fred. He had tiptoed down to the basement to filch a fifth of vodka.

Fred always had trouble sleeping, especially when he was sober. The problem got so bad that he asked Bobbi if she had any medicine that could help him. She gave him a prescription from which she had had excellent results. Out of curiosity she looked it up in a physician's desk reference, which said: "Caution: Could cause priapism in men."

A couple of days later she said, "That pill was pretty good for you, huh?"

"Best night's sleep I've ever gotten."

"Did you notice anything different?"

"Yeah, jeez, I had the biggest hard-on for a couple of days."

Two or three weeks later a woman came to visit Fred. "Hey, Bobbi!" he shouted just before her arrival. "Got another one of those pills?"

It was just before and during Fred's time with the Reidels on Wellesley Island that one of the happier events of his late years took place: his younger daughter, Alexandra, reentered his life. For the first time he got a taste of what he had missed in fatherhood. He did not prove a natural at it, but he mixed fatherhood and Fredness in a way that pleased her greatly.

By the mid-eighties Nancy felt that Alexandra needed Fred. Nancy's marriage to the physicist in Texas had ended. He had adopted Alexandra when she was four years old, but the two had never become close. Now he was gone. In 1983, when Alex was fifteen, Nancy wrote to Fred: "This has been a difficult year for [Alex] . . . She *needs* a father. I'm not asking you to step in and fulfill this role at this point, but if the two of you could establish a relationship where at least there could be some communication, I think it would help her."

So Fred invited Alex to spend some time with him in the Bay. In a state of high nervous excitement, she flew from Dallas to Syracuse, clutching a copy of one of his books; she needed his dust-wrapper photograph to recognize him, it had been so long since they'd seen each other. The plane landed in Syracuse but no one was there to meet her, so she started walking through the airport. Suddenly she heard a male voice shouting, "Alex! Alex!" She looked around. There was Fred, sitting at a bar with Clark Reidel.

He put her up at the Edgewood; he was still at the trailer with Clark and, now, Bobbi as well. The resort had a waterside cottage where summer help sometimes stayed; it was empty, so Alex was allowed to use it. She had a splendid time. She went to family picnics with Clark and Bobbi, or made the rounds with Fred. He introduced her to everyone he knew, invariably getting the same response: "Oh, Fred, I didn't know you had a daughter!" For hours she sat beside him at Cavallario's, nursing her club soda, listening to the bar talk, feeling thoroughly grown-up. He loved to tease her. Because she'd traveled a fair amount for someone her age, he called her The Little World Traveler. One night he decided to spring for dinner at Cavallario's. "Order whatever you want!" She wanted surf and turf. When the waitress came over he said, "The Little World Traveler here is going to have surf and turf, but I don't have that much

211

money, so you'd better bring me a meatball." For the rest of the summer he rode her about that, the surf and turf and the meatball.

There was one unsettling incident. A few days before Alex was to return to Nancy, the Edgewood moved her into a regular hotel room. She hadn't seen Fred all day; when he came to her room he appeared to be drunk. He started asking her questions about what her life had been like when she was a little girl; while she told him, he kept trying to apologize for not having been there with her. Then he said, "Why don't you just lie down with me? I just want to hold you like a little girl." She was shocked and started to cry. So did Fred. That opened the gates. They began to talk more intimately and honestly than they ever had before, with no barflies around to get in the way. By the end of the evening Alex felt she knew her father far better.

In 1985 Nancy decided to leave Texas and move back to New York State. She and Alex stayed with Charlotte for several weeks. Charlotte had been ill, but her good spirits were undiminished. She hauled out scrapbooks and photo albums that gave Alex a sense of her father's family for the first time. She didn't see Fred every day, but they always spoke on the phone. One night Fred came to the house drunk. He shouted to Charlotte, "Get those Goddamned people out of the house!" Nancy and Alex were behind a locked door. "What are you doing, cowering in there," he shouted. "We're not cowering," Nancy replied. Finally he broke the lock and started swinging at her. Alex, a strong, determined girl, jumped between her parents, screaming, "Don't you ever touch my mother!" She took a mighty poke at Fred's chest. He grabbed himself, staggered against the wall and moaned, "You got me right in the fuckin' nitro patch!" For weeks thereafter he made the rounds, telling everyone at every bar in Alex Bay how his kid had hauled off and walloped him. He loved it.

Later that year Nancy bought her house in Cuyler, but Alex wasn't ready to live there. She moved back to Texas for a year, then came to Cuyler. During her senior year of high school Fred was on her constantly about going to St. Lawrence University in Canton. Maybe he wanted her near him, maybe he liked the school because he was known and admired there. Whatever the explanation, he pressed the argument relentlessly. When Alex told him in midsummer of 1987 that she still hadn't made up her mind, he got mad. Over the phone he shouted, "Haven't you decided what you're going to do with your life *yet?*" Then he hung up. The next time they spoke was five months later. Alex was in her dormitory at Emerson College in Boston when the phone rang at four in the morning, waking all her roommates. She got on the line. Fred said, "Did you catch that Giants game tonight?"

While she was in college Alex met her future husband, Ken Mowers. He was a construction foreman in Cortland, which irked Fred no end: the great egalitarian thought that someone who worked with his hands was unworthy of his daughter. By then he had moved back to Alex Bay, and offered her "any books, pictures, the desk on which I wrote the trilogy, and so forth." The only stipulation was: ". . . do not bring Ken up here. I'm not going to be such a hypocrite as to tell you on the one hand that your marriage to a construction worker has no chance whatever, then pretend that Ken and I are bosom buddies. You, your mother and I can load a pickup if you borrow one. I want you to consider this gift my graduation present." Eventually she took Ken to meet him anyway. When they arrived Fred said to Ken, "Drive me to the grocery store and we'll get some steak," and to Alex, "Clean my apartment while I'm gone." They stayed away for hours. When they finally returned, in a liquefied state, they were the best of friends.

Alex and Ken were married in Cazenovia in the fall of 1990. She wanted nothing more than to be given away by her father. He hemmed and hawed, but finally said he would get back from a trip to London in time to fulfill his fatherly duties. A couple of weeks before the wedding a woman called from London and told Alex: "Your father's really sick, but he's going to be there. He wanted me to call and tell you this. He's really sick, though." That was no lie; the London trip was Fred's last fling, and he paid dreadfully for it. But the truth was that standing up in public was something Fred was constitutionally incapable of doing for his daughter. A couple of days before the service he called Nancy to promise he'd be back in time, but she knew him better than their daughter did; she arranged a stand-in, a family friend, for him.

On the wedding day people from Watertown and Cazenovia were there, but Fred was not. One of his friends told Nancy he had had congestive heart failure, which was true. But the real reason he had gone to London in the first place was to escape an obligation—a responsibility—he simply could not discharge. Alex was deeply wounded, but she refused to let her unhappiness alienate her from her father, especially once she realized how serious his illness really was.

If that trip to London in 1990 was the beginning of the end for Fred—he had less than two years left to live when he returned—a trip to that same city four years earlier, paid for with a large chunk of his Guggenheim money, had been a bravura exercise in Fredness. It failed to produce the stories about Michael Herr and Sarah Miles for which *Rolling Stone* and *Esquire* had hoped. But it gave Fred great pleasure, and it permitted him to add a few footnotes to his legend.

London in 1984 was a lark for Fred, though the trip started on an unpromising note. Fred had been sober for several months, taking his daily walks, playing golf at the Thousand Island course, writing late at night; he felt that *Last Notes from Home* was just about wrapped up. Clark and Bobbi Reidel drove him to Toronto to catch his British Airways flight; he was carrying his bag and wearing a little cap, looking for all the world like a boy being sent off to school. The Reidels went to the gate with him, then retired to the nearby hotel where they were spending the night. Around eleven o'clock the phone rang. It was Fred, and he was hammered.

"Fred," Reidel asked sleepily, "what's going on?"

"Oh, God damned British Airways," Fred said. "They want to put me up at some cheap motel here. See if you can get me a room there at the Plaza. Flight's been cancelled. Can't get out until tomorrow morning. I met this guy, a travel agent, and we've been at the bar having a couple of vodkas."

A couple of vodkas, indeed. Fred had fallen off the wagon with a colossal thud. That was the way it went. He never planned to fall back into the drink; if anything, he may have wanted to stay sober and productive. But a little change in his routine or his plans, something frustrating and irritating, was all it took.

He arrived at the Craven Garden Hotel in London much the worse for wear, so much so that the woman at the desk found it difficult to believe the disheveled wreck before her was the noted American writer the hotel was expecting. But soon Fred had her transfixed and was droning sweet nothings in her ear. She was waiting for her Prince Charming. "Until he gets here," Fred said, "couldn't we just. . . ."

Soon Fred went off on his appointed rounds. Michael Herr interested him less than Sarah Miles, but he made the effort. He found Herr, an American who had moved to England, at his house in Kensington, in an inhospitable mood because a previous encounter with the press had not gone to his liking. It turned out that he and Fred had met previously at the Lion's Head and that they shared an upstate connection, so they soon found common ground. They took a walk together, in the course of which Herr suddenly felt hungry. The place where they stopped had an all-too-familiar look. "Jesus Christ, Herr!" Fred complained. "My first meal in London and you drag my ass to *McDonald's!*" They then boarded a bus for a tour of the city, but were kicked off after Fred began interrupting the guide's spiel and laughing at inappropriate moments. Fred enjoyed his time with Herr; his pleasure is reflected in the piece he wrote, but as the editors who read it pointed out, the piece is about Fred, not Michael Herr, and it is far short of first-rate Fred.

Sarah Miles was another matter: a beautiful, sexy movie star, formerly married to the eminent playwright and screenwriter Robert Bolt, whom Fred held in high esteem. He talked with her at her house in Notting Hill, and had a separate interview with her ex-husband. Bolt had recently suffered a severe stroke, but Fred was able to talk with him about *Lawrence of Arabia, A Man for All Seasons* and other matters of mutual interest; Bolt was "a hulking, extremely handsome and modest man of sixty with a graying, neatly cropped beard, both a gentle man and a gentleman."

Sarah Miles was a more delicate business. Though friendly, she was "playing movie star for me, and . . . in the grand manner." First "she'd called and demanded to know how I'd had the balls to make an appointment with her ex-husband . . . without allowing her to make the arrangements." Then she failed to set her clock when daylight saving time ended and missed an appointment with Fred for drinks, dinner and an interview. Finally they did talk at her house—he was taken aback by its modesty and ordinariness—where he had three vodkas over the course of the afternoon. When he started to pour another, she "snatched the bottle, forcibly screwed the cap back on and put it back in the cabinet." It was "all I could do to restrain myself from rolling around the floor laughing and crying, 'Sarah, old buddy, when I'm on the stuff I can do a bottle and a half of that a day and still remember what you tell me.' "

Toward the end of Fred's six-week stay in London he was joined by the Reidels. Arriving at the Craven Garden, they found that Fred had set himself up as king, and was adored by every bellman and chambermaid in the hotel. All three of them had round-trip tickets that had been purchased far in advance at a low fare, but Bobbi—whom Fred liked to call Baba—was having a wonderful time shopping and decided to add a couple of days to their stay. When British Airlines informed her that there would be an additional charge for changing the departure date, she told the agent, as Fred wrote, that she and Clark "have been sent over on an errand of mercy to retrieve an American writer of 'national renown,' one who is a hopeless alcoholic off on a bender someplace but that she's sure I'll turn up momentarily and that one of the reasons for my trip was to interview Peter O'Toole, with whom I've become quite chummy and who of course does TV commercials for BAC."

The ploy worked. Fred and his friends were able to delay their arrival at no additional cost, but the Reidels warned Fred that a surprise awaited him on board the plane. In response to a query Bobbi had said that a wheelchair would not be necessary for the alcoholic author, but the airline representative volunteered that he would be served no alcohol. Fred was furious. He had injured a tooth in a London cab and badly wanted anesthetizing:

By this time my tooth is killing me, for the London "dentist" has claimed to have killed the nerve only to have my own guy tell me he'd only partially done that and that I couldn't have made it without vodka, so that in the back of the cab I'm now telling Baba, while Clarko is laughing like a madman, that if I don't get a drink I'm going to boot her ass the entire 180 miles from Toronto to Alexandria Bay. . . . Aboard and airborne, the flight attendant asks if I'd like wine with lunch, I sigh with relief, order a double vodka, borrow a couple five-mg. valiums from Baba, take them with the vodka (it is time to sober up anyway, get to my own dentist and get some words on paper) and drift slowly down thinking of Sarah and Robert.

Once he was back in Alexandria Bay and sobered up, Fred had to face the unpleasant reality that *Last Notes from Home* was not quite as wrapped up as he had imagined it to be. He wanted nothing so much as to finish it and get it into print, so that the trilogy—his life's work—would be complete. The idea of a trilogy had been suggested to him by David Markson. In the mid-seventies Fred showed him the draft of a screenplay he was working on about his brother, Bill. Markson told him this wasn't material for the movies but for a third volume that could serve as counterpoint to the first, setting up a revealing contrast between the two brothers.

Markson thought that sandwiching *Pages from a Cold Island* in the middle of a trilogy might help redeem it. He didn't much like Fred's second book, but, like all of Fred's friends, couched his criticism in positive terms. He felt that by comparison with *A Fan's Notes,* "the emphasis is much more on externals, Wilson, Steinem, etc." rather than on Fred himself. He had "an interesting notion that if, in the third volume, there's more Exley pain, more episodes in his own head (so to speak) than in terms of seeking meaning via others, it will throw *Cold Island* into an entirely new focus, maybe make it the capstone of the three." This last obviously was said in hopes of bolstering Fred's self-confidence, but the rest of Markson's commentary was right on the mark, as Fred seemed to understand. He worked hard to make the most out of what he may well have known would be his last book; though he fell far short, his effort was admirable and should not go unremarked.

He began the book in the mid-seventies on the Hawaiian island of Lanai, staying with Jo and Phyllis Cole; in *Last Notes from Home* they are affectionately portrayed as Wiley and Malia Hampson. Lanai was "perhaps the last of the unspoiled islands—no motels, no bars, hence no tourists— and still twenty minutes from Honolulu by Cessna." In February 1975 Fred wrote to David Markson that he was "utterly sober, working, sunning and walking the beach." He knew "how hardly I've used myself and want more than anything, before I go see Big Daddy in the Sky, to finish the trilogy that *you, David,* put into my head." There was nothing feigned about this. Every friend of Fred's was aware of how urgently the concluding volume of the trilogy pressed itself upon him, and how afraid he was that he would not be able to finish it.

Random House wanted the book finished too. Its investment in Fred was significant, though that was not the most important consideration; it had recycled Fred's first two books into Vintage, Ballantine and other subsidiaries, and had gotten back some of its money. Nor did anyone at Random House think that Fred was taking the firm for a ride, hitting it for advances and then not doing the work to which he had committed himself. By comparison with many other writers whose big advances had not produced books, Fred was small potatoes. Bob Loomis knew that Fred wanted to finish the book far more than Random House wanted to see its investment in him bear fruit; it was for Fred's sake that he was worried, not for his own or his firm's.

For Fred the problem wasn't putting the words on paper, it was making them hang together. By 1979, four years after starting work on the book, his struggles had only begun, as a letter from Loomis dated February 5 indicates. He had just read a section in which a number of the book's characters were introduced:

> Your curse is that you can write about just about anything with interest. . . . I can't honestly say that I understood your point about it all, though, and I can see why it was a very difficult chapter to write. It's really not an easy one to read, either. It's sort of like trying to pull up a thin root in the grass. You think you've got it and then it takes off in another direction. Then you think you've got it again and it takes off once more. Perhaps the cohesiveness of all this suffers simply because it comes right after that really marvelous chapter about Ms. Robin Glenn. . . . But as I say, Fred, you can get me interested in just about anybody. Somehow, though, as smoothly as you work from one character to the other, I personally began to resent being yanked from one to another and without any clear idea of just why or what it was all about until almost too late.

"I hate to write you this," Loomis added, "because I know you're working hard and well, but I hope you want me to say just what I think—always." The truth is that Fred wanted quite the opposite, the praise that he always needed.

Five years later he sent a section of the book to Markson—the one about the girl who offers herself to him and whom he subsequently betrays—which he said was "I think the most powerful writing I've ever done," a plea for praise the response to which has been lost. Two years after that, in May 1986, Loomis again had to couch criticism amid compliments: "The ending to Book Three is terrific (there are a few sentences here and there that I couldn't quite follow, or which seem to me to be repetitive in structure with some other things, but the life, and feeling, and style, and humor are all there in abundance)," and two months later he added: "It's great seeing all of this together. I hope by this fall you'll have finished, and we can schedule the damned thing."

The fall of 1987 was more like it. Fred had held onto the book for more than a decade, writing and rewriting, perhaps fearful of letting it go and then facing judgments not merely about the book itself but about the trilogy as a whole. By November 1987, though, Random House had the completed manuscript in hand and was ready to publish it. Considering how long it had waited, its decision to put off publication for nearly a year—nine months from acceptance of a manuscript to publication of the finished book was publishing's norm—was not without its ironic aspects, but it made sense. Loomis told Fred he faced "a long wait, I know," but "the problem is not production but rather preparing, as best we can, for the book." This was the sales department's argument, and Loomis found it convincing. Rushing the book out in the spring of 1988 would not "give us anywhere near enough time to do everything we can, and would like to do." Holding off until September 1988 would permit time to distribute bound galley proofs as widely as possible, accompanied by copies of *A Fan's Notes* and *Pages from a Cold Island,* "hoping for some reviews which will take into account the trilogy." Loomis was sympathetic with Fred's impatience, but firm. He "could muster no arguments" against the sales department's case: "We simply can't give the book every chance if we publish before September, and since most major orders are written up for all the titles on the spring list in the first week of December, I think the sales force would be very uneasy trying to deal with *Last Notes* that early."

There was an additional problem as well, one that had given Harper & Row pause two decades earlier. In January 1988, Loomis asked Fred to go through the manuscript "and note all the characters and tell me which ones are real, and if they are real, what their real names are, and so forth." He was "worried about privacy (and to a lesser degree, libel)," and he wanted to avoid getting lawyers involved. A case involving another Random House book, a biography of J. D. Salinger by the British writer Ian Hamilton, was winding through the courts, focusing on the issue of whether a biographer could quote unpublished words without permission; publishers were nervous about legal issues of privacy that had not previously concerned them.

Fred and Loomis settled the matter by telephone. By spring the book had been set in type and bound galleys had been assembled. True to Loomis's word, Random House was making a major effort in behalf of a book the sales prospects of which were dicey at best. It ordered a first printing of thirty-five thousand copies—a big one for an author whose sales to date had not matched his reputation—and it had an advertising and promotion budget for the book of twenty thousand dollars, the lion's share going to *The New York Times Book Review* for a full-page advertisement. The publicity department was hard at work, the principal result of its efforts being a story in *People* magazine; Fred may have groused about *People* and the celebrity culture it both spawned and catered to, but he was grateful for the attention.

The book that emerged from all this labor, apprehension and delay is the longest volume in the trilogy. It opens with the news of Bill's inoperable cancer. Fred plans to visit him and cannot prevent Charlotte from joining him. The airplane flight to Hawaii gets the book off to a promising start. It introduces two of the book's principal characters, the first a garrulous Irishman named James Seamus Finbarr O'Twoomey, the second a flight attendant named Robin Glenn. The former is a comic figure whose darker aspects emerge as the novel progresses. The latter Fred calls "perhaps one of two women he'd ever love," but it is not a simple passion. If on the one hand Robin offers in her "lovemaking . . . something wild and intelligent and abandoned and imaginative and rather terrible as opposed to the awful sincerity of so many women," on the other hand she "lied about everything and it wasn't so much that she didn't care what these tales might do to another as that she was totally oblivious to the irreparable damage her meretricious slanders were initiating." Robin appears to be a pastiche of several of the women Fred had known—it cannot be insignificant that he gives her his second wife's maiden surname—with everything built to heights of exaggeration, or fantasy.

At Bill's funeral a new character enters the story, a friend from upstate named Toby Farquarson III, a man's man and ladies' man about whom Fred fantasizes as well. If Robin is the ultimate woman, at once seductress and betrayer, Toby is the man that Fred himself was not: contemptuous of the conventional world yet at ease in it, able to thumb his nose at the same time that he makes his own swaggering way.

The last of the major characters to appear is Alissa, a psychiatrist to whom Fred's confessions occasionally are addressed. Fred has "always had this dream of the two of us ending together, married, and in the hope you'd have the son you've always professed to have wanted, despite having turned down at least three guys I feel would have been perfectly suitable." This is yet another fantasy, connected with "this sappy vision of finishing the third volume of my trilogy, having it come out to great acclaim, realizing that this in turn would send the readers, in droves, back to the first two volumes."

At this point the book turns into pure fantasy and, for the first time in Fred's life as a writer, pure fiction. O'Twoomey kidnaps Fred and holds him captive on Lanai; from that point there is nothing of note in the book's central plot that bears any discernible relationship to anything that actually happened in Fred's life. He is on his own, the raw material of his life utterly depleted, and the book falls to pieces. It is a sign of his desperation that he digresses from the story of Fred and Robin and Toby and O'Twoomey and inserts two completely irrelevant sections, "In the Days Before I Shot My Sister" and "Blowjob." The first is barely fictionalized; the precise source of the second is unknown, but presumably it is based on something in Fred's past that troubled him.

The book lurches from one improbable event or disclosure to another. Robin turns out to have a profitable prostitution racket on the side, O'Twoomey is an arms dealer and

Irish Republican Army agent; when he carries Fred off to Lanai, it is with the aim of getting him off alcohol and forcing him to finish *Pages from a Cold Island*. It all ends with Fred's marriage to Robin and his closing declaration: ". . . I shall in the end defeat you, Miss America, shall defeat you, learn to live with you, and make you mine."

The book has a great deal of energy, contains some vivid writing and at times is funny in Fred's characteristically raunchy way. As Bob Loomis pointed out, Fred had real skill at bringing characters to life and making them interesting. The O'Twoomey business goes on too long, but Fred gets this loquacious fraud down exactly right. Robin Glenn is less successful, primarily because everything about her is so outsized that nothing about her is believable; she is a cartoon, which presumably is not what Fred meant her to be.

The greatest problem with the book, though, is the same one that *Pages from a Cold Island* suffers from: it has no center. Fred tried manfully to put Bill there, to employ the contrast between the brothers as a metaphor for American attitudes toward warfare and then to use Bill's disaffection over Vietnam as a way of bringing the brothers together at the end. But Bill gets lost in *Last Notes from Home* just as Edmund Wilson gets lost in *Pages from a Cold Island*. Fred had nothing arresting to say about either of these men and nothing further to say about himself, or at least nothing worth writing about. *Last Notes from Home* is a better book than *Pages from a Cold Island* if only because it is more ambitious and less gratuitously vulgar. But the main effect of both of these books is simply to announce that they are the work of a one-book writer.

The reviews of *Last Notes from Home* were sympathetic and friendly if on the tepid side. Christopher Lehmann-

Haupt of *The New York Times* took note of prose that "has gone soft in places" and "raucous boasting," but said that "his music of angry contempt and self-loathing, for all its obscene sentimentality, still holds its quavering melody." Paul Gray of *Time* said that Fred "again demonstrates his skill at hallucinatory free association" and urged him not to stop at a trilogy but to "go for a tetralogy." Other judgments of a generally favorable nature came from *The Village Voice,* the *Chicago Tribune, The Boston Globe* and *The Washington Post.* Writing in *The New York Review of Books,* Thomas R. Edwards was one of the few reviewers to view the trilogy in whole and at length, on balance treating it with respect. Only Dan Cryer of *Newsday* was able to separate his admiration for *A Fan's Notes* from his dislike of *Last Notes from Home;* he deplored Fred's "often bloated, undisciplined prose and his vain—no matter how tinged with self-loathing—gaze into the mirror," and lamented his "self-regard and self-pity." He came closer than anyone else to the truth.

Last Notes from Home did not fulfill the expectations Fred or Random House entertained for it. Early sales were promising, but before long returns started rolling in. Vintage brought it out in paperback and still keeps it in print, but it is *A Fan's Notes* that puts Fred in the bookstores. He thought that as the final volume of his trilogy, *Last Notes from Home* would bring him the recognition that was his due, his entitlement, and he awaited a Pulitzer Prize. Random House nominated the book, but any book can be nominated by anyone willing to pay a small fee. Fred's chance at fame in the terms that meant most to him, the respect of the community of serious writers and readers, had come two decades before. He had been rewarded with a fair measure of what he desired, so it is too bad that he longed for a mere award as reaffirmation of what he already had.

Fred's health was bad and his morale was not much better. If he had quit writing with the completion of the trilogy, no one would have been surprised. Yet he kept at it, dogged as ever in his fashion. He wrote one last piece for *Esquire,* one for *GQ,* and he started work on a novel that—this was his latest and last fantasy—he firmly believed would assure his fortune.

His piece for *GQ,* a portrait of the Lion's Head, has already been quoted from extensively; *GQ*'s editors were eager for respect in the journalistic community as well as for readers seeking advice about fashion and sex, and they published Fred gladly, in their December 1990 issue. His last piece for *Esquire,* published a year earlier, described his infatuation with Diane Sawyer, of ABC News, and his meeting with her at Mel Zerman's apartment in New York. The piece has acquired a place in Fred's mythology all out of proportion to its merits, which are slender.

"I love her, I worship her, she's my goddess!" That's what Fred had told David Hirshey at *Esquire* in 1984. Sawyer was a woman of beauty and intelligence, if not taste: early in her career she had worked for Richard Nixon, whom Fred despised. If anything, this made her seem all the more mysterious, which simply intensified Fred's obsession with her. He was shy about approaching her, as he was shy with most women, but when he finally got through and asked her for an interview, not merely was she agreeable, she was willing to meet him at Zerman's apartment. They talked briefly there. She had to meet her husband and left early, passing through the building's empty lobby: "As fate would have it, the doorman was answering nature's call and missed her exit." When Zerman returned the next morning after a brief hospital stay, he exchanged pleasantries with the doorman and asked how long Sawyer had stayed. "She... she... she's still up there" was the reply. Later, in her office at ABC, Fred told her, "For two minutes, Diane, I was the biggest make-out artist in New York." She laughed and said, "Savor it while you can, Fred."

Fred got a modest amount of mileage out of that story, but his hopes were invested in a manuscript called *Mean Greenwich Time.* It was to be "a spy thriller," about "a 43-year-old English professor whom the intelligence community won't leave alone." In his last years he talked about it constantly. He thought that what he'd written "is pretty funny"—it isn't—but claimed that he would not cheapen his literary style in order to cultivate the masses: "It's like a guy trying to make a lot of money by suddenly deciding he wants to write like Judith Krantz. You can't. Judith Krantz, she's such a... moron. She believes everything she writes. Or like Sydney Sheldon—they're the ultimate fantasy." Still, his book was going to be a big best-seller, a piece of commercial fiction that would play to the market and rake in the big money that his more serious books had never come close to earning.

At the time of his death Fred had completed fifty-six double-spaced pages of the book, which he sometimes called *Hemingway's Last Muskie Run.* That title is drawn from the alias given to an agent who was to have a prominent role in the story: "If thirty-five years of inebriation had devastated

Hemingway's other gifts, it had not destroyed his loyalty to his friends, or theirs to him. Wherever he went, Venice, Kenya, London, Princeville, Alexandria Bay, Auckland, Alice Springs, and no matter the state of his alcoholic stupor, his wide toothy grin was invariably met with laughter, embraces, *Saluds,* and chants of *Hem, Hem, Hem.* Hemingway loved and was loved."

What Fred was doing is transparent bordering on embarrassing. Not merely was he paying tribute of sorts to Ernest Hemingway, he was wrapping himself in the mantle of Papa. Though he may have thought of this book as fiction, it clearly was to be yet another contribution to his own mythology. This is further suggested by the only complete chapter he wrote, which focuses on a larger-than-life Thousand Islands fishing guide named Addison "Ad" Baudine, shaped in the same unconventionally heroic mold as Toby Farquarson III of *Last Notes from Home.* Ad Baudine is another of Fred's fantasies, based not merely on a friend from Alexandria Bay but also on Ernest Hemingway. It cannot be coincidence that Baudine is dying, and dying well; Fred's own mortality was much on his mind, and he wanted to go out with dignity. There is no way of knowing how he would have developed the Baudine fantasy had he been able to finish the book—an incomplete outline that he left gives no hint—but past performance leaves little doubt that it would have been along lines flattering to himself.

The few thousand words of this manuscript have no redeeming qualities. Apparently Fred believed that Hemingwayesque prose as well as a Hemingway persona was the key to commercial success, for he abandoned the rich, meandering style that is his trademark and affected a truncated style in the Hemingway manner. The imitative effects are heightened by the emphasis on fishing and boats and manly strength, not to mention dropping in a bit of French every now and then. The connection between this manuscript and *A Fan's Notes* is so thin as to be invisible. Over the years confession and self-abnegation had become bluster and self-promotion. Fred, perhaps mercifully, had no understanding of this at all.

THE LAST YEARS OF FRED'S LIFE WERE LONG AND SLOW. With his writing going so poorly and his little world gradually falling apart—his years on Wellesley Island ended, his mother and aunt died, his illnesses became more and more severe—time must have weighed heavily upon him. Yet life had its pleasures. Returning to Alexandria Bay, he resumed his old routines and delighted in them, as well as the attention that fell to him as a consequence of his local renown. In addition he closed his own small circle by reconciling with his elder daughter and by meeting the first of his grandchildren.

"I'm on a death watch for my mother," Fred said from time to time in the late 1980s, but he was better at talking about Charlotte's failing health than he was at doing anything to help her. In her last months she gave up the house on Walton Street and moved into an apartment that her sister had set up in her own house on Crossman Street. Finally Frances Exley Brown came to get her mother, and took her to her house on Washington Island a few miles away. It was there that Charlotte died, on October 22, 1989. She was eighty-three years old. To everyone who saw him, Fred seemed the same as ever, off in his own universe. Surely he felt grief, if only of a purely selfish nature; he no longer had "Mom" to do his bidding. But he remained silent, keeping whatever feelings he had to himself.

At the time of his mother's death Fred was still living with Clark and Bobbi Reidel on Wellesley Island. He stayed there until the summer of 1990. With Clark struggling to reestablish himself after losing his job, things weren't quite the same on the island. Fred was also beginning to worry about himself. He wanted to be closer to the hospital in Alex Bay, so he took over the space his mother had just vacated and moved in with Aunt Frances. For a small sum he sold "all the contents and furnishings of my Wellesley Island apartment" to Clark Reidel, except for "the correspondence and manuscripts in the cardboard box beneath my desk and those books especially requested by Peter Dzwonkoski."

Fred was drinking less now than in the past, and sometimes went for weeks without alcohol, not because he was writing but because medical necessity was finally, belatedly, impressing itself upon him. Frank Cavallario, who in the past had let Fred's tabs soar into the ether, now did not hesitate to cut him off. He worried that Fred was trying to kill himself with booze, and gently told him, "Freddie, you've had enough."

Still, the world of drinkers was where Fred lived. "My social life is circumscribed within the length of a football field, with The Ship restaurant on the east, the Dockside at midfield and Cavallario's Steak House in the western end zone." Not long after that was written a couple of other places, the Admiral's Inn and Bootlegger's, were added to the circuit. He made his rounds like a physician on call or a pilgrim doing the stations of the cross. Depending on what schedule he was on at the time, he started either in the morning or the early afternoon, moving regally from one bar to the next, sitting in his own seat at the bar, running each tab up a few more dollars as he nursed a vodka or—more often in those years—a low-alcohol light beer. He talked endlessly, spewing opinions and insults in every direction, pausing every few sentences to make sure people were listening—"Right, Jack?" he'd ask. "Don't you agree, Buddy?"—before plunging onward. He was in a town and region he cherished—he thought it was the most beautiful place in the world, and couldn't imagine why anyone would want to live elsewhere—and among people who cherished him. A visitor from the outside captured him in his place in just a few words:

> It was his friends that really pulled the whole thing together. . . . It was because of their generosity and love, and in the midst of their accomplishments, that Exley functions. He is their childhood friend and gadfly, constantly deflating their pretensions (and they are not pretentious people: they are, in their own way, *classic,* cranky and chauvinist upstate Irish and Italians; the very same folks who spawn the jocks who turn into people like Exley); and to them he is a constant and well watered reminder of the perils of sensitivity and the intellectual's life.

Fred made his rounds on foot. He drove a car only if he had no other choice. In 1987 he bought a 1974 Oldsmobile for six hundred dollars. His next car was a 1973 Pontiac Bonneville, inspiring John Golden, a columnist for the *Watertown Daily Times,* to call him "downwardly mobile." That car didn't last long either, for in August 1989 he purchased from Henry Rouse, a prominent local businessman, a 1981 Dodge Omni "for the sum of one dollar ($1.00)," fair value for any Omni of any vintage. The handle on the driver's-side front door was broken, but Fred knew just how to fix that; whenever he wanted to go somewhere, he climbed in through the window. Mostly, though, he stayed out of cars because he knew he was likely to get in trouble behind the wheel. That is exactly what happened in the winter of 1989, when police in Alexandria Bay pulled him over and accused him of driving under the influence, not to mention failure to give a signal, failure to observe a stop sign and failure to dim his headlights. When the police stopped him, they demanded that he recite the alphabet.

This was the ultimate insult. Recalling the incident for John Golden, Fred waxed ever more indignant. The cops were "just trying to humiliate me," he said. "They were glowing. Here's that guy who wrote those books they don't understand. As far as not reciting the alphabet, after all, I've been nominated for an NBA, I've won the Faulkner Award, I won the National Institute of Arts and Letters Rosenthal Award, and so I just started laughing to myself. Of course, I didn't know then the guy who was asking me to recite the alphabet spelled *failure* 'f-a-i-l-o-r.' I'd have arrested him for failure to spell." How much had he had to drink that night? "I only had two." Was he drunk? To quote "the great Rocky Graziano, when asked by Johnny Carson if he'd ever thrown a fight, 'Not that anybody can prove.' " The authorities, Fred said, were "serious about the drinking." He added: "I'm serious about it, too."

Then he actually did turn serious. "I have very long periods of sobriety," he said. "I'll probably work all summer. I'll probably have to go down to New York this summer to do a piece on Diane Sawyer. I might have a couple down there. But I won't have a drink until—[I] don't know—fall." He realized that the past was catching up with him. "I haven't reached a point yet where I've had to be confined," he said, "but I can see that coming unless I watch myself very carefully. I reached a point where I don't even like alcohol. I don't drink for enjoyment.... I don't like the taste any more."

When Fred went to London for a second time in the summer of 1990, the trip had no apparent purpose. The members of his family assume that it provided a convenient excuse for Fred to get out of the commitment he had made to give Alexandra away at her wedding. It served that end, but Fred paid a high price for escaping his paternal duty.

Fred was sick when he reached London and he got much sicker while he was there. He looked awful. He went to Harrods with a stunning woman who turned people's heads as she strolled through the store. When they left he said, "All those people looking at you, they must have been thinking, what on earth is that beautiful creature doing with an old stumblebum like him?" She replied, "Oh, Freddie, fuck 'em. You're my friend and I don't care."

Suddenly he was back in Alexandria Bay, two weeks earlier than scheduled. Frances had been driving along when she saw a stand where raspberries were for sale. She bought some for Aunt Frances, who loved them, and detoured through the Bay to drop them off. When she entered the house, her aunt said, "Fred's back." Fran was astonished. "He's not supposed to be back for two weeks." She walked back to his room, took one look at him and said, "Fred, you're going to the hospital."

"No, I'm not," he said. "I'm not going until after the football game tomorrow."

"Fred, there's not going to be any tomorrow. You're going now."

Fran called Clark Reidel. She asked him to come over to get Fred dressed and help her take him to the hospital. He was there shortly. They got Fred to the emergency room. His alcohol level was sky-high. He was put on a respirator, which gave Fran an unwelcome chill. It was a year to the day since their mother's death, and she never wanted to hear that respirator again. The doctors told her that Fred had a respiratory disease, and that it was fatal.

A few days later Gordie Phillips came up from Rochester to visit his old friend. He was concerned about the quality of the care Fred was getting at Alex Bay, all the more so when a nurse told him that if anyone in her family was there, she "would get them the hell out of there as soon as possible." After hearing that he drove to Cape Vincent and urged Fran and Irwin to move Fred to Watertown; he said he would be happy to pick up the tab for any expenses this entailed.

Fran subsequently took Fred to Watertown and registered him at the Good Samaritan Hospital. There he was diagnosed with congestive heart failure and put in the care of a cardiologist. He was forced to withdraw from alcohol and nicotine; he had been smoking three packs of cigarettes a day. To ease his withdrawal, he was given massive doses of morphine. That had a calming effect, but not totally. He cursed and swore at the nurses, and spat at one. When Gordie dropped by a few days later, he took this as a sign that Fred was becoming his old self, which was confirmed when he told Fred that he was going to pay for his relocation from Alex Bay to Watertown. Fred winked, smiled, and said, "Not to worry, chum. It was a free ride."

Soon Fred was back on Crossman Street, where the situation continued to deteriorate. Aunt Frances wasn't in great shape herself. Every thirty seconds she asked what time it was. To drown her out, Fred had the television set on at high volume. For three nights in a row, he didn't sleep. He found beer in the refrigerator and drank it. He needed further medication, but a doctor in town refused to give him any. Fran found another, who prescribed a mild sedative; before then Fred had been on Serax, which helped lower the pandemonium inside his mind and memory and thus made it easier to stay off alcohol.

That was in the fall of 1990. When Fred finally got back on his feet he took on a role previously unknown to—and presumably unimagined by—him. He became the caretaker for his failing aunt. The time had come to repay the devotion to him and his siblings of this woman who, childless herself but blessed with modest wealth, had supported them in numerous ways. Fred's nursing talents were limited, but he was happy to make coffee in the morning, do some of the shopping, and keep Aunt Frances company. The one thing he declined to do was to get her ready for bed; he claimed that he didn't want to embarrass her.

Each morning a young woman came by to tidy up the place and check on both of its rather helpless inhabitants. Connie and Fran visited daily, often for hours at a time. Connie and Fred had never been close, but they started to find things to like about each other. She often brought him food. He protested, "You don't have to do that!" "I don't have to," she said. "I want to." She and Frances could tell that Fred was drinking again, but he was allegedly a grown-up and there wasn't much they could do about it that hadn't already been done.

Word of Fred's illness got around quickly. Inexplicably, he told a few friends in New York City that he had lung cancer and had only a short time left to live. What is interesting about this fantasy is that complications from lung cancer were the cause of Earl Exley's death. Nothing is to be gained from reading excessive psychological import into this parallel, but Fred's apparent yearning to pattern himself after his father yet once again is, at the least, noteworthy.

One of those who heard the bad news was Fred's daughter Pamela. She was by then thirty years old and had straightened out her life in a thoroughly satisfactory way. In college she had dropped out to get married and had a daughter, Ashley, but within a year and a half she and her husband had been divorced. A couple of years later her luck had changed for the better. She had met and married Dan Anderson and had her second child, a boy named Austin.

Pamela had turned into a self-disciplined young woman, stable and solid. She knew little about her father and his family, and wasn't at all sure she wanted to know any more. But she was Exley to the core. More than a decade earlier she had been in Miami at art school. Connie and John O'Neill were there on vacation. They tried to get in touch with her, but without success. Then one day their son Patrick was riding to Miami Beach with friends. They saw a car with Connecticut license plate "EXLEY.1," overtook it and looked in, "and there was a girl with a face just like

Uncle Fred's." Connie tried once more to reach Pam. They got together for dinner and had a good time, but fell back out of touch. This did not discourage Connie. She took photographs of the cousins Pam had never seen; when no one came to the door at Pam's house in Darien, she left the pictures in the garage, with an explanatory note.

Pamela learned about Fred's heart condition. She didn't know what to do. She had a powerful impulse to turn away. Her few encounters with her father since her parents' divorce had not gone well, and she had no idea how he would receive her. Her mother had always told her how nice Fred's family was, but she didn't think the Exleys were really interested in her, Connie's behavior to the contrary notwithstanding. She had a good life and had no desire to disrupt it; if there was one thing that Fred could be counted on to bring into someone else's life, it was disruption. But it remained that this was her father, he was gravely ill, and it was hard for her to do nothing. She was a strong person, but she was not hard-hearted.

So she called Connie and asked for her advice. Connie said that the doctors were giving Fred three years to live and urged her to come up for Thanksgiving. She felt that seeing Pamela would be good for Fred, and that it would be good for Pamela herself as well. Pamela was still reluctant, but her husband took up Connie's side of the argument. He told her that if she didn't reconcile with her father before his death she would regret it ever after. She was grateful for his counsel and finally decided that he was right.

She drove to Alexandria Bay just before Thanksgiving. Not merely did Dan, Ashley and Austin accompany her, so did Francena. As it turned out, the visit was more a reunion of husband and former wife than of father and daughter.

Francena had very much wanted to see Fred. Over the years their connection had never entirely dissipated. Fred called Francena every few months and they corresponded from time to time, though they hadn't seen each other for about fifteen years.

Fred met them in the lobby of their hotel. He took them to Aunt Frances's house, where they sat and talked for a while. Most of the conversation was between Fred and Francena. Pam was tired and felt she was in the way, so she and her family went back to the hotel. Francena stayed for a couple more hours. When she returned she said she was happy to have seen Fred, but she was shocked and dismayed at how much his condition had deteriorated.

Thanksgiving dinner was held at Frances and Irwin's house in Cape Vincent. Plenty of Exleys were on hand, and Pamela soon found herself welcomed into their midst. Fred was usually ill at ease among young children, but he relaxed; the rest of his family was friendly, talkative, entertaining. For the first time in her life Pamela began to realize what she had missed. However unresolved her feelings were about her father, she was glad she was there.

A few weeks later Fred drove down to Greenwich. He stayed at Francena's house—separate bedrooms—and saw Pam daily, either at her house or at her mother's. He wasn't drinking, which made it easier for her to be with him and to talk to him. He had brought along a bunch of his clippings and other mementos, and scrapbooks in which to paste them. She was pleased and touched. It was obvious that this was her father's way of telling her that she mattered to him and that he wanted her to know what he had done with his life, that he was respected and liked by people whose opinions allegedly mattered. She had tried to read *A Fan's Notes* when she was in college, but had put it aside because she found it so depressing. Now she felt mature enough to read it, which she soon did with sympathy and admiration. She understood that Fred saw and felt things more keenly and deeply than most people do, and that this was essential to his accomplishments as a writer; this made her regret all the more the abuse to which he had subjected himself, and the lost opportunities this entailed.

Fred stayed in Greenwich for a week. He and Francena got along well, but a week was as much domesticity as he could take. He left, but his renewed relationship with Francena revived his old affection for her, at least to some degree. After he returned to Alexandria Bay he called Pamela from time to time. He asked her to keep a close watch on her mother, because he was afraid that Francena was vulnerable.

Pamela never saw her father again. They kept in touch, but she was busy and he was burrowing in for his final siege. In 1991 she became pregnant again. Her third child, Anna Rae, was born on June 7, 1992. Pamela spoke to Fred from the hospital the next day. It was a happy conversation. He was eager to see his third grandchild. It was the last time they talked.

For Fred it was a long stretch of last times. He made a final visit to New York City. He stayed with Mel Zerman and made his usual forays to the Lion's Head. One night he was in the dining room and his still-attractive former inamorata Alice Denham was at the bar. She waved at him. "Well, Freddie, hello!" He peered at her dimly, befogged by alcohol. "Who's that old bat?" he asked.

There was a final visit to Gordie Phillips. Fred stayed at his old friend's house in Rochester. His fire was out. He sprawled on the sofa and rarely left it. They talked in the usual way, but Fred's heart wasn't in it. He went back home, then telephoned a few days later.

"I'm not going to last long," Fred said.

"Freddie, cut the bullshit," Gordie replied. "Stop feeling sorry for yourself. You'll probably come to my funeral."

"No, I'm sick."

He was. He talked about death more and more. He and Bobbi Reidel made a pact that if one was seriously ill in the hospital, the other would read passages of poetry and prose that he or she was fond of. Fred mentioned works by Emily Dickinson, Dylan Thomas, Alfred Lord Tennyson and others. Yet even if he was in a lugubrious cast of mind, he hadn't given up. He often talked with Clark Reidel about going to Cleveland to undergo experimental surgery to strengthen his heart. The arrangements got fairly serious, but nothing came of the idea.

One day in the spring of 1992 Fred called his old friend Leo Dephtereos in Watertown. They hadn't seen much of each other for a long time. Fred had abandoned his old hometown—driving past on Interstate 81, he rarely pulled off to enter Watertown, unless it was to pick up pasta at an Italian grocery he'd patronized for years—but Leo had stayed on, faithfully running his family's restaurant, the Crystal. When Fred telephoned, it was to say good-bye. "I probably won't see you again," he said.

ON JUNE 8, 1992, FRED WAS IN A GOOD MOOD. FRAN AND Connie were with him in the house on Crossman Street, sorting out the immense pile of belongings that Aunt Frances, a pack rat, had left when she died in December 1991. The task was so daunting that they had made no attempt to do it all at once; instead they decided to stretch it out over several weeks. Fred was chatty and upbeat. He volunteered that he was going to ease off the vodka and beer. He was getting puffy and was concerned that the Lasix he was taking to reduce the excess fluid in his lungs would also elevate his potassium and cause heart problems. He was determined to look after himself, and faced the task cheerfully.

Pam called during the day with news of Anna Rae's birth, which further improved Fred's spirits. Fran and Connie were working in another room, but he repeatedly urged them to come into the living room to watch *Every Which Way But Loose,* a Clint Eastwood movie he'd rented so many times that he knew it almost by heart; he recited some of the dialogue along with the actors, laughing at himself as he did so, and pointed out little details in the film that his sisters would never have thought to notice. He talked about resuming golf, taking up the Thousand Islands course on its offer of free play when he was sober.

Fran didn't see Fred the next day, Tuesday. On Wednesday morning she went out for groceries. As soon as she returned her next-door neighbor ran out to tell her that a nurse in the emergency room at Alexandria Bay was on the telephone at his house; Fran's phone apparently was not working. The nurse told her that Fred was in the hospital and in bad shape. He had refused at first to be put on a resuscitator, insisting that any decision be delayed until Fran got there; she would decide. Fran was stunned, because she knew that Fred was well aware she had been unable to make exactly the same decision in behalf of her mother or her aunt. As upset as she was, she was coolheaded enough to realize that Fred was just being Fred, letting someone else assume responsibility.

This is what had happened. Sometime during the previous afternoon or night Fred had gotten up from the living-room sofa, apparently to close the back door against the late-day chill. He fell on the coffee table and broke a drinking glass. He tried to get a blanket—he was wearing only his underwear—but couldn't reach one; in that attempt he cut himself on shards of broken glass, and he accidentally hit the OFF switch on the television set's remote control. He was in utter darkness, unable to move, with no hope that anyone would come to the house before nine o'clock the following morning. He never talked about that night, but it must have seemed to last forever and it must have been terrifying. His head was flat on the floor; as his lungs filled with fluid it became harder and harder for him to breathe. Surely he thought he was going to die.

The young woman who kept an eye on him stopped by at nine-fifteen on Wednesday morning. Fred could talk but not move. "Just call Clark and have him come get me," he mumbled. Instead she called an ambulance. When the crew arrived the situation seemed obvious. With vodka bottles all over the place and an old man slurring his words, what they had was someone who'd had too much to drink. They assured the woman that Fred would be all right.

At the hospital it was quickly determined that he had had a stroke. Fran got there as soon as she could. Fred looked up at her from his bed and mumbled that he was scared. He told her that over and over. When his oxygen mask was removed momentarily Fran saw that his left eye and the whole left side of his face were lifeless. The doctor told her that he was paralyzed on his left side and probably would never walk again.

By the weekend Fred's condition had stabilized and his mood had improved. On Saturday night he asked Fran to bring him a fresh strawberry yogurt, which she promised to do the next day, but when she left home at seven on Sunday morning no stores were open. She told him that she would bring him the yogurt that afternoon, but he was not placated. He was furious. He told her to "get the hell out of here." Those were the last words he spoke to her.

Fran went to a telephone and called Connie, who had rented a cottage nearby for the summer, and asked her to bring the yogurt. It was an ethereally beautiful day. Fran went back to Washington Island. Her children and grandchildren came by to visit. It was a happy family occasion that she did not permit Fred's outburst to spoil, though she was heartsick over it.

In the early afternoon Fran called the hospital. She was told that Fred had been given Librium and had finally calmed down. She decided that since she had upset him so much in the morning it would do neither him nor her any good for her to return, so she stayed at home.

Fran spent much of the rest of the day worrying about whether Fred was aware that he had had a stroke and whether he understood its potential consequences. She assumed that he knew because nurses and doctors kept testing his reflexes, but he had never said a word about it to her. She feared there would be no alternative to placing him in a nursing home, and she knew he would hate her forever if the decision to institutionalize him fell upon her. He would be a terrible patient, demanding and abusive, and the staff of any such place would find him a handful.

Early that night she received another call from the hospital, this one from Fred's doctor. Fred had suffered a second stroke and was now in a coma. His temperature was a hundred and five; he was wrapped in a coolant blanket. Fran rushed to the hospital and stayed with him all night. Irwin was with her, and so was Connie. The next morning, on her way out of the hospital to freshen up and rest, Fran spoke to the nurse who had been with Fred during the previous day. The nurse told her that Fred had asked for her in the afternoon. No one had called to tell her; the intensive care unit was unusually busy and no one had a chance. This was hardly Fran's fault, but she felt a rush of guilt that never thereafter left her. Her brother had asked for her and she did not come. Was he angry at her right to the end?

Fran returned to the hospital on Monday. She was there for nearly two days, sitting by Fred's bedside in the intensive care unit, catching a quick nap on a chair right outside the door. Bobbi Reidel came to visit. She sat by Fred's bed and read aloud the poems and other pieces Fred had said he liked. This alarmed Fran and Connie. They knew that Clark and Bobbi had been loyal and self-sacrificing friends of Fred's, but they feared that this literary exercise was doing their brother no good; they also thought it was bizarre and macabre. They insisted that Bobbi leave.

The last hours of Fred's life were excruciating for Fran. As she sat by his bedside she could see the gauges measuring his pulse rate and blood pressure steadily fall. The life was literally draining out of him. At nine-thirty in the morning, June 17, 1992, Fred died.

His will was brief. It had been written in 1984 and was never revised. Fred made "no provision" for Pamela and did not mention Alexandra. He left all of his property, such of it as there was, to his two sisters. He had originally specified that he be cremated and his ashes "dropped in the Lost Channel of the St. Lawrence River," but in the fall of 1991 he changed his mind and asked to be buried next to his father and mother in Watertown. This was done.

Ten days after his death a memorial service was held for Fred at St. Mary's Catholic Church in Clayton: an Episcopal service presided over by a female minister in a Catholic church in memory of an unbeliever. Fredness to the end. Before his death he had stage-managed it down to the last detail. He wrote down a list of people whom he wanted to be notified; among them were both of his former wives and many people whose presence in his life he had treasured, including Lynn Nesbit, Bob Loomis, David Markson and Frank Gifford. He also chose his pallbearers. They were all men, and they were all from upstate.

On the afternoon of Saturday, June 28, 1992, they stood there in honor of their old friend, the boys of Watertown High School. Jack Scordo, John Doldo, Leo Dephtereos, Gene Renzi, Gordie Phillips. Ashes to ashes, dust to dust:

Everything goes back to Watertown.

Watertown Daily Times

ACKNOWLEDGMENTS

I am grateful beyond measure to Frances Exley Brown, Fred's twin sister and executor, whose cooperation with this book was freely given and unstinting. Fran spoke with complete candor about her beloved brother, granted me full access to his and his family's documents, and encouraged many others to cooperate with me. I could not have written this book without her help.

Everyone else in Fred's family was friendly, informative and helpful in numerous ways: his sister Connie; her husband, John O'Neill; Fran's husband, Irwin Brown; Bill's widow, Judy Exley; Fred's second wife, Nancy Glenn; and his two daughters, Pamela Anderson and Alexandra Mowers. I am grateful to, and fond of, all of them.

The contributions of certain of Fred's friends and associates are clear in the text, but I would like to make special mention of Gordon Phillips, Jeanne Adams Harris, Lynn Nesbit, Bob Loomis, David Markson, Clark and Bobbi Reidel, Mel Zerman and Jerome Raskin. All of them helped me fill some of the blank spaces in some of the most important periods of Fred's life. Others who talked about Fred to useful effect were Will Blythe, Mike Bresnahan, Jr., Frank and Connie Cavallario, Alice Denham, Leo Dephtereos, John Doldo, Peter Dzwonkoski, Sheila Fallon, William Fallon, Barbara Hendra, David Hirshey, Eugene Renzi, Robert Renzi, Henry Rouse, Paul Scanlon, Jack Scordo and Jann Wenner. Small but important contributions were made by William Gaddis, William H. Gass, Les Krims and John D. Weaver.

Jann Wenner at *Rolling Stone* and David Hirshey at *Esquire* permitted me to walk off with files of Exleyiana that proved of incalculable value; I am grateful for their kindness and their trust. At the *Watertown Daily Times* its managing editor, John Johnson, Jr., provided unlimited access to its excellent files, and Elizabeth Hatch helped me find my way through them; John and his wife, Susan, became my friends. At the University of Rochester, Peter Dzwonkoski opened all the doors I needed to enter and then left me alone, a rare and precious favor; I am also grateful to Mary Hutch, Jean Lombard, Suzanne Schroeder and Evelyn Walker of his staff.

Readers whose curiosity has been aroused by the wholly admiring portrait herein of Robert D. Loomis are hereby assured that every word of it is true. Bob was the editor of my first book, and returning to his fold after an absence of two decades has been for me the happiest aspect of writing this book. I warned Bob in advance that he would be editing a book in which he played a prominent and flattering role. He allowed as how he could live with that.

It was Liz Darhansoff, my agent, who got me to Bob in 1974 and got me back together with him in 1994; thanks for that and for everything else, over all these years. Three of my favorite people—Marie Arana-Ward, James Conaway and Edwin M. Yoder, Jr.—provided helpful advice and comment at various stages in the book's evolution, as did both of my sons, Jim and Bill. For the first time in my sporadic book-writing career I managed not to inflict too much of this work in progress on my wife, Sue, who was all too engaged with her own business. But as always, she was there when I needed her.

—Jonathan Yardley
Sand Cove, Maryland
May–September 1996

About the Author

JONATHAN YARDLEY is the book critic and a columnist for *The Washington Post*. He is the author of four previous books, including *Ring: A Biography of Ring Lardner* and *Our Kind of People: The Story of an American Family*, and the editor of *My Life as Author and Editor*, by H. L. Mencken. In 1968–69 he held a Nieman Fellowship in Journalism at Harvard University, and in 1981 was awarded the Pulitzer Prize for Distinguished Criticism. He lives in Baltimore and Cecil County, Maryland, with his wife, Susan Hartt Yardley.

About the Type

This book was set in Granjon, a modern recutting of a typeface produced under the direction of George W. Jones, who based Granjon's design upon the letter forms of Claude Garamond (1480–1561). The name was given to the typeface as a tribute to the typographic designer Robert Granjon.